The Other Front In Afghanistan

Stories of Maiwand

Building Governance and Development

CARLOS TERRONES

Copyright © 2012 Carlos Terrones

All rights reserved.

ISBN: 1479233900
ISBN-13: 978-1479233908

Disclaimer:

The opinions and characterizations in this text are those of the author, and do not necessarily represent official positions of the United States Government. The Department of State completed the review of this book and has no objection to its publication.

DEDICATION

To my family, friends, and girlfriend, thank you for all the support you provided me during my tour in Afghanistan.

To my Afghan counterparts, thank you for believing in our team and me.

To my military counterparts, thank you for all of your great support.

To the State Department, thank you for providing me with the opportunity to serve in Iraq and Afghanistan. I will always cherish this experience.

To my close colleagues in Afghanistan, thank you for all of the support you provided the DST.

CONTENTS

	Acknowledgments	i
I	Reconstruction	1
II	Decision and Preparation	8
III	On the Brink	20
IV	Road to Recovery	92
V	The Last Push	131
VI	Transition	175
VII	Post Maiwand	192

ACKNOWLEDGMENTS

To Patrick Rankin for editing the book.

I

RECONSTRUCTION

These stories describe my experience in Afghanistan. The Afghan war not only has the military component but also the civilian component, where policymakers like myself are embedded on the front lines fighting the war to bring governance and development. This is the "The Other Front In Afghanistan."

By 2010 the future in Afghanistan looked bleak. President Barack Obama's civilian-military counterinsurgency strategy was about to change with an increased numbers of civilians who would be embedded on the front lines to assist in repairing the fragile state of the war-torn nation. The Taliban fighters were getting ready for their massive Spring campaign and civilian experts with Iraqi experience like myself extended our duty of service to serve Afghanistan. Assistance was needed to revamp the civilian efforts to build governance and economic development. I put on my bulletproof vest again and signed up for my Afghan tour. I came into an awkward situation in a district where I didn't feel welcome, one that was on the brink of collapse. A district known as the birthplace of the Taliban, where relationships were broken between the District Government and the District Support Team (DST). A district where the civilian-military relationships were broken. A district that didn't receive much international aid assistance. A district that was forgotten.

It was a cloudy and rainy day when a U.S. Army Blackhawk helicopter dropped me off in the Western side of Kandahar

Province in the District of Maiwand, in a small Combat Operation Outpost (COP). The only guidance that I received from my superiors was "Go to Maiwand and see if you can make something happen. No questions asked. See if you can do it." The only things that I brought to the front lines to assist our Afghan counterparts were my pen, notebook, and knowledge. With no real guidance on what to do or how to fix the state of the Maiwand District and with minimal resources, I was about to go into a situation where I confronted many challenges. I will take the reader on a journey where you will be able to learn from my personal and professional experience in trying to turn Maiwand around.

My book is not about the philosophy and theory of the war. I would like it to be used as a handbook for practitioners before they go into the field and for students at graduate schools so they can learn from my experience. I've been doing international development work for several years in Latin America, the Middle East, Eastern Europe, and Asia. My specialty is building government institutions in emerging democracies. I have worked closely with foreign government officials on local public policy. I have a strong personality and relish the challenge of solving difficult problems in troubled areas. It was the situation in Afghanistan, however, that drove me to write this book. I am an optimist, and this quality allows me to find ways of making governments function better. Doing good governance work in war zone environments, such as Iraq and Afghanistan, is not easy. Many factors, such as security and civil unrest, can complicate building a local institution. But I made a difference in Afghanistan, if only for the short-term. I say short-term because the environment in Afghanistan doesn't allow you to determine if your success can be sustainable. In places such as Maiwand, one of the birthplaces of the Taliban, success is determined only if Afghans are willing to take the lead after we leave. We made progress in Maiwand during my tour and if our Afghan colleagues continue to build on the success that we achieved as a community, then we could have a long-term success.

The book includes stories as well as details of technical work that I did in the District of Maiwand. In each chapter, you will learn about our projects and how we turned around Maiwand. I go back and forth with things that I've discussed previously in other chapters. The idea of the book is to take you on a journey from how I began to how it ended. Due to the nature of my assignment I will not reveal the real names of the people I worked with and met in Maiwand. They have fake names but they are real people, and I developed a strong connection with my colleagues and with the District Governor (DG) of Maiwand. You will also get to know my personal side, which I can't separate from my experience. Living in the conditions and what I dealt with on a daily basis was difficult. I sought strength and courage many times through my girlfriend, Cynthia. She was a big part of my tour in Afghanistan.

Later, I will take you through a series of examples of the work I've done in the District of Maiwand. We had a good team and were in charge of governance and development. The most important challenge personally was when I was tasked to save Maiwand from collapse. I may be exaggerating a bit by saying "collapse," but the situation in Maiwand wasn't good when I arrived in the district. I developed many strategies but, with strong leadership, I got the district on the right path.

Those who might be interested in my book should treat it as non-fiction. It chronicles my time in Maiwand and ends with my reflections on my last days in Afghanistan. Again, I will go back and forth to several items, so it is important to pay attention to the terminology. The book flows chronologically, like a diary. I tried to strike a balance between challenges in my daily existence living in such a foreign place and analyses of the professional challenges I faced. I included strategic frameworks that I developed and we employed in our district and how we were able to improve it. I put a lot of focus on management and leadership, two important elements needed to push policies on the front lines. With the book I tried to deliver the message that we could win the hearts and minds of the populace and we could work together with the community, which in the end would benefit the Afghan people.

My stories from Afghanistan will shed light on how I prepared mentally and professionally in order to succeed in my position. My preparation was a key factor to insure that I would have no regrets as I got ready to leave Afghanistan. I hope international development practitioners and policymakers can learn from my experience. It was important that I did my homework before I accepted this type of assignment, especially when I knew that people depended on me for solutions.

As I start to write these stories, Afghanistan remains the talk of nation building by the United Nations, United States, European Union, and other coalition partners. Granted, the economic woes in the West might have put the Afghanistan talk on the back burner. I am not sure how appreciative the Afghan government has been for the U.S. assistance. President Hamid Karzai sometimes sends messages that call into question the Afghan government's support for U.S. assistance. We implemented good projects but sometimes it felt as it was never enough for our local Afghan counterparts and I understood their frustration. Afghanistan is a unitary system and, in districts like Maiwand that are far away from Kabul, residents feel they are part of another country. We as a team did our best to mentor and work with our Afghan counterparts but, in the end, I felt that I left the country frustrated. I don't know what the future holds for Afghanistan. The country is not moving forward as it was supposed to. Policies are not well developed and we need to continue with good mentorship. I needed patience to mentor my Afghan counterparts, and sometimes I felt like I was walking into a brick wall because they wanted us to solve all of their problems and do everything for them.

I worked in Kandahar Province, known as the birthplace of

the Taliban. In Kandahar we have a large international coalition force, which combines military and civilian experts. This is not an all-American led effort. Policymakers made some mistakes, like building schools without teachers. We will continue to make mistakes and this is the reason why I am writing this book: to add to our lessons learned so we can succeed in Afghanistan. We have funded projects to alleviate the problem in the short-term but we need to think in the long-term. The U.S. Agency for International Development (USAID) developed a District Delivery Program (DDP) to assist with the filling of the government civil servants positions in the district. In Pashto, the civil servant government staff is known as "Tashkiel." We provided a large amount of aid to subsidize the cost of this program to increase the salaries of Afghan employees to work in a district. This is a good USAID program that helps with the problem in the short-term but it is up to our Afghan counterparts to take a greater lead and make it sustainable for many years to come.

As I start to write my stories, Afghans are getting ready for the poppy harvest season. Poppy planting season takes place in the Fall and then harvest starts in the Spring. Poppy cultivation is big business in Afghanistan and injects a large amount of money into the Afghan informal economy. Additionally, it is a major income source for the Taliban. Unfortunately, the Afghan government hasn't done anything or much to provide a long-term sustainable agriculture program for the farmers in Maiwand, which would allow them to grow legitimate crops. It is important that we provide good mentorship to our Afghan government counterparts in order for them to develop a good sound policy that will deter farmers from cultivating poppy. I never heard of one while working in Maiwand. Too much emphasis has been placed on eradication, with no clear alternative livelihood plan that would convince a farmer to not plant poppy. A couple of wheat seed donations are not adequate.

America is currently undergoing economic challenges and the

American people want the economy to be fixed. Even if we execute a quick, massive pullout and focus on our own backyard, the Afghanistan war will have a place in history. I don't know how historians will write about the Afghanistan war. What my eyes saw can be of interest not only to those who work on policy for Iraq and Afghanistan, but also to the random citizen in order to understand that we also have civilians embedded in the front lines fighting this war.

I don't believe a democratic system can be built in the short-term. It takes years for a representative government to develop. In countries like Afghanistan that have gone through cycles of intervention and violence, we should be more patient. We have spent centuries advising emerging economies and countries at war on how they can do better policies. It is important that we don't create a donor dependency trap for Afghanistan, dissuading Afghanis from becoming their own agents. I don't think there will be another large operation such as what we have experienced in Afghanistan. I hope that we have learned our lesson if we are ever going to intervene in a large nation building operation again. An arrogant belief to know what is best for a country without studying that country's culture could backfire. This arrogance would call into question the quality of a policy. History will determine and decide if the Afghan war was worth it or not. The policymakers who were involved in the original intervention probably have their own opinions on how history will write about Afghanistan. However, people like me who were on the front lines and experienced the challenges and struggles of implementing policy at the ground level have a different perspective and opinion.

Afghanistan has taught us that no matter what we do and how much money we spend in nation building, we can't expect to see productive results in the short-term. There are countries that can be fixed quickly while there are others, like Afghanistan, where productive outputs may come much slower. I am not sure about the future of Afghanistan; it really worries me. As you read my stories, you will learn that we probably made progress in small pockets, like Maiwand. However, it is unfortunate that the successes that we had are only short-term. We need to make it more sustainable and have a long-term policy for the good of the people in Afghanistan.

As much as we tried as a team, our success depends on the Afghans. Sometimes our Afghans counterparts don't want to accept the reality that as part of the post-2014 transition our security presence will shift to a supporting role; whereby, the Afghan National Security Forces (ANSF) gradually assuming full responsibility for security across the districts. A strong security will complement the governance and socio-economic development in the districts. I don't believe that it is too late to fix Afghanistan. With the proper policies we could still make it work. Good lessons learned will be part of the success.

II

DECISION AND PREPARATION

It was the Spring of 2010 when I began to reflect on my experience in Iraq and thought about whether I should continue to do reconstruction and development work in conflict nations. During that time, I had heard a substantial amount on Afghanistan. It was the primary talk on the news, as Iraq became a lower priority. By 2010, Iraq was becoming more stable and I had a feeling that there was more to be done in Afghanistan. I felt I had some energy left and that I could take on another assignment. Just as I wanted to see what all the fuss was about when I applied to work in Iraq, I was curious to see what was going on in Afghanistan. I've always had this adventurous feeling inside of me that drove me to do this type of work. I didn't know what to expect from Afghanistan, although the thought of this country made me a bit nervous. Before I decided to apply to another assignment, I read a lot about Afghanistan. I kept reading about all the casualties and that the major push for the U.S mission would be in late 2010 with a large civilian surge. I knew that if I were to apply, I would be part of this major push by the U.S. in order to bring stability in Afghanistan. I read a lot about Kandahar as the birthplace of the Taliban and how the Taliban destabilized the province. I learned about the low literacy rate, high unemployment, poppy production, and, most importantly, the large insurgent activity. When I was about to leave Iraq in 2010, Iraq was more stable and there was a sense that progress could be made. I began to see progress in Iraq since I landed in Baghdad in 2008. I worked in the Sunni Province of Al Anbar and I completed my work in the

Shiite province of Diwaniyah. I was engaged in building the local institutions and provided economic reconstruction development. Among the U.S. soldiers in Iraq, the talk began about Afghanistan. We all knew where the action would be. We knew the world's eyes were on Afghanistan, and that people like me might end it up there. Many of my friends told me to come back home to restart my life in America. Life and work was difficult in Iraq, and I had second thoughts about my decision to go to Afghanistan. But I didn't listen to those who love me and went forward with my decision.

When I came back to Iraq from America in the late Spring of 2010, I looked at the jobs advertised and found several positions available for Afghanistan. I wasn't wrong when I foresaw the big push for a bigger presence there. If I were to make some type of impact on local policy, I knew the State Department would provide me with that opportunity, as it did in Iraq. I am very grateful for the opportunity the State Department allowed me to have because I've learned so much about how to build governments. I knew that if I were to engage directly with local officials, a State Department assignment was the best fit. I received an email from the State Department advertising governance advisors positions to work in the field. I finally decided to send my application almost two months before I concluded my tour in Iraq at the end of July 2010. The application wasn't difficult because I knew I had the background and expertise. Also, I knew that I had my security clearance, which would make it easier to move me from Iraq to Afghanistan. By mid July, only three weeks before I was scheduled to complete my tour in Iraq, I received an email from Human Resources accepting my application. The letter specifically said that training and departure to Afghanistan would start in August 2010. I knew they would take my application but I didn't know how quickly they wanted me to go to Afghanistan.

I worked in Iraq from 2008 until 2010. I knew I needed some time to decompress before taking the job in Afghanistan. I was a bit burned out from Iraq and wanted to spend some time in

America. I declined the State Department offer and told them that I could start in the Fall of 2010. There were no issues with my security clearances; the toughest part was getting into the right training class. I was also informed that I was going to work at a District Support Team (DST) in Shah Wali Kot. I had no clue what a DST was. I only experienced working for a Provincial Reconstruction Team (PRT). The PRT is a team composed of civilian-military experts engaged in reconstruction work. I searched on the Internet about the DST but didn't find much. I think at the time the DSTs were still evolving. I researched Shah Wali Kot and I found out that it was located in Kandahar Province – the birthplace of the Taliban. How funny things are. I read so much about Afghanistan when I was in Iraq before I applied and I knew Kandahar was probably a place that I didn't want to go. Now I knew I was scheduled to go there. It was a dangerous assignment but I had to adapt and agree to go where there is the most need. If the U.S. mission needs you in a specific district or province, you just go and don't complain. I never tried to seek comfort in this type assignment; I knew that it would be difficult. I knew that sometimes you are thrown into an assignment and literally you are on your own. This is the reality on this type of work, sometimes you are send to a district or province, without guidance and objectives, and you could find yourselves trying to find out what you really need to do the first six months of your assignment. By the time you finally realize what you need to do, your tour is up. It happened to me in Iraq and I didn't want this to happen again. I did my homework before I went to Afghanistan because I knew my training in Washington might not be enough.

By late October I began to prepare myself mentally and emotionally. Thanksgiving was around the corner and I knew that Thanksgiving in 2010 would be my last one in America until probably 2012. When I looked at my one-year assignment and possible Rest and Recuperation (R&R) breaks, I knew I would be spending the 2011 holidays in Afghanistan. When I worked in Iraq,

I didn't take that many R&Rs, which was probably a reason why I was burned out when I completed my tour. Working with the State Department, I was allowed to take three R&Rs for two weeks each. I promised my girlfriend, friends, and family that if I was to go to Afghanistan I would take all available R&Rs, making my tour in Afghanistan easier. Having worked in Iraq, I didn't think I had the energy to make it in Afghanistan with only one R&R. I kept my assignment secret. In the early Fall 2010, many of my close friends and relatives kept asking about my future plans. I never really went into details but my brother had this intuition that I would go to Afghanistan. When October came and everything was finalized, at a family dinner, I told my family that I was leaving soon for Afghanistan. They were very worried because they kept hearing violent news. They were not surprised that I was going to go. I had built this reputation among my loved ones that, if there were a major war out there, at some level, I would get myself into it. I told my family that I have the energy to do one more tour in Afghanistan. Afterwards, I would come home for good. When I started in Iraq I was getting close to my mid-thirties. By the time I was heading to Afghanistan, I was getting close to my early forties. Deep inside, I did a lot of reflection and knew that I didn't want to spend more than a year in Afghanistan.

Working in a conflict zone could be emotionally draining and difficult. There are people that go to work in conflict zones because of the financial gains, love of adventure, or wanting to make a difference. I really enjoy working in the field. I always had this feeling that I wanted to help the people that had nothing to do with the war. When I began to think about my upcoming assignment, I began to think about the many days and nights that I would spend alone. I was told that I wasn't going to be in a large base. I knew that I would be somewhere working on the front lines away from the large bases. I pictured the worst as I prepared for anything. I lived in very bad conditions in Al Qaim, Iraq and I began to think of the same living conditions. I tried to search for pictures of small bases in Afghanistan in Kandahar Province. The living conditions in small Combat Operation Outpost (COP) bases didn't look that great. However, based on my experience, I also considered the possibility that I may end up going somewhere else, possibly up north. If I was to go to Northern Afghanistan, I was going to be faced with very cold weather. For my original assignment, Shah Wali Kot, I didn't find many pictures online, and the little I found depicted Spartan living conditions.

Once I started to move away from the possible living conditions, I began to focus on the real work: building governance and development in rural Afghanistan. I studied the country in detail, just as I had in Iraq. By early November, the State Department had already informed me that I was scheduled to report to Washington right after Christmas. My training would start right after the New Year and I would fly to Kabul in the third week of January 2011. At that moment the adrenaline began to kick in and I knew there was no time for regrets, just to move forward with the decision I made. Life has put me in situations where I had to make critical decisions and go with the best intuition possible, and I have grown as a person because of it. I knew Shah Wali Kot was just around the corner.

To be ahead of the game in terms on the work I would do, I began to research how the Afghan government works, as I think it is important for folks that work in conflict zones to do their homework before they go to an assignment like Afghanistan or Iraq. I am a strong believer that it is important to manage your knowledge well, which would help you to avoid risks. I began to read reports on Afghanistan written by the World Bank, Think Tanks, Military Experts, United Nations, and other U.S. Government Agencies. The majority of the contents included raw data, personal and professional experience on how experts experience rural and urban Afghanistan, the economic and government challenges, and also the culture norms. It is important to adapt well to the local culture. I read a lot about corruption and the high illiteracy rate. This was part of the Afghan culture and I knew I had to adapt to reality. My knowledge of Afghanistan prepared me to picture a possible realistic picture on what I could achieve in the field. I tried to focus on reports from military and civilian experts that described their one-year or many years of experience living and working in Afghanistan. I always compared reports to see similar accuracy. I also read blogs written by the military and by reporters. By reading their experience on the ground, I visualized better what I could expect. I placed a lot of emphasis on reading on how the Afghan government works. I read the sub-national government law and the roles of the provincial and district officials. To my surprise, I found some of this information directly from the Afghan Ministry websites and available in English. Because I knew I was going to work in local governance, learning how the government worked was important. I wanted to be ahead of the game because once you reach the ground, you could find yourself overwhelmed with too many demands by your local counterparts. This is a basic tool that I recommend someone do before they deploy to a high stress-working environment: Do your homework.

If you didn't take the time to learn how the government system works you could find yourself wasting resources while trying to do something that may never work. If you really want to try to make a difference in the short time you would be in post, then you need to be ahead of the game. You would waste your time if you wait for people to tell you what to do. Unfortunately, I have seen many civilian experts just learning how the system works towards the middle of their tour, or at the end. You have to think strategically and do a basic SWOT analysis - I sought Strength, Weaknesses, Opportunities, and Threats on what I could accomplish while in the field. This self-learning process served me well throughout my training. By early December, after reading so much about Afghanistan, I had an idea on how the Afghan government works. I knew Afghanistan was a strong unitary system, that the President had a lot of control over the appointments of government officials, and that District Governors didn't have much of an influence over local politics as they were appointed and not directly elected. I didn't know if I was completely accurate in my learning process, but I knew that once I reached Afghanistan I would compare what I read with actual experience. But having some basic knowledge on the country's economic and political hurtles was important for my familiarization.

By mid- December, I began to feel a bit nervous, as I knew Afghanistan was just around the corner. I was getting ready to report to the State Department. I had to think what I was going to take to Afghanistan. As with Iraq, I planned to pack light. However, packing for Afghanistan during the wintertime meant heavy winter clothes, especially if I didn't really know where I would be assigned. As I already mentioned, your original assignment might change as soon as you report to the U.S. Embassy in Kabul. So I knew I had to be flexible. Packing light really prepared me mentally to know that I would be going for a short-term and that I would be coming home soon for a break. It is a mental preparation strategy. If you pack a lot, you could vision yourself to be in Afghanistan longer and that could make your time go slower. I was going to travel with my small Patagonia carry on. Below is the list of items I packed:

- One winter coat
- Six black t-shirts
- Six pairs of underwear
- Seven pair of socks (three gym socks and four winter socks)
- One pajama pants
- One cashmere black sweater
- One winter hat
- Two pairs of shoes (winter desert boots and sneakers)
- One belt

- One scarf
- One pair of gym shorts
- One pair of winter gloves
- Hygiene products

As you can see, I travel very light. The other things that I took with me were my laptop, vitamins, flash drive, IPOD, and headphones. I don't know why I have a tendency to wear black t-shirts when I am in the field. With all the dust, I should have worn something different but I still wore black t-shirts. I did it in Iraq when I first arrived back in 2008 and I am wearing one as I am writing these stories in Maiwand. They were easy to replace when I went on vacation. People told me to not bring brand name clothes, but I did anyway. It is important to feel comfortable with what you have and wear. I also packed light because I knew once I reached the U.S. Embassy I was going to be issued more items. The State Department sent me a list of possible items that I was to be issued once I reached the U.S. Embassy. If you added that to what I was bringing, plus the protective vest, it was a lot to carry around, especially when traveling by air in a helicopter. Wearing a protective vest could add extra pounds, and in the summertime it gets very uncomfortable because you sweat like a waterfall. I didn't have to buy much before I began to lay out what I was going to bring. I only knew I had to buy black t-shirts. The last time I wore them was in Iraq. I knew that after I completed my tour in Afghanistan, I would not be buying black t-shirts for quite a while. Once I had everything that I could possibly need, it was time to start packing. I knew that I was going to be moving around for almost a month and a half. Below is my traveling itinerary before I knew I was going to settle in my district:

- Travel to Washington, DC. last week of December,
- Travel home to spend New Year's,
- Travel back to Washington DC and stay there the first two and a half weeks in training,

- Travel to the Training Center for a long week civilian-military training in mid-January,
- Travel from the Training Center back to Washington, DC for a three-day weekend and get ready to travel to Kabul, Afghanistan,
- Travel to Kabul and stayed at the U.S. Embassy for orientation the last week of January, and
- Travel to Kandahar Air Field (KAF) Area A and then to the Kandahar Team (KT) in Kandahar City for one day. From there, I finally made it to the District of Maiwand. (I never ended up going to Shah Wali Kot. I will explain later the sudden change in my assignment, which was not unexpected.)

So yes, I moved a lot before I reached to my final destination. It was very tiring to go through all of the above changes because not only was I in motion in training but it was difficult to adjust to the thought that I was going to Afghanistan in the first place. I guess now you understand why I travel light.

After Christmas, it was time to travel to Washington, DC. I reported to the State Department and the orientation process was almost the same as what I went through when I departed for Iraq. It was just typical procedures like any other employer makes you go through. I did my payroll, got the proper identification cards, filled out health forms, and discussed my benefits. We had a small group and this group would accompany me all the way until I got to the U.S. Embassy. From there, we were all going different ways. I was going to spend some time with these individuals, a medium-sized group of people with different backgrounds. Some had Iraq experience like myself, while others came from the NGO sector, military sector, or U.S. Government agencies.

We were told to come back the following week after New Years and get ready for a long training course. The courses were brutal because they didn't seem to add much value, especially for those that already had the experience working in the field. So much content was thrown at me that it was hard to absorb everything, and we had a long schedule. We discussed and listened to topics such as how the U.S. Government Agencies work in Afghanistan, expectations, and brief language training. We also had speakers who had just come back from the field.

One interesting anecdote that I will never forget from this training is that by the second week, everyone at the class was talking about their districts. We were provided with a map of Afghanistan with the U.S. presence in the field. When I looked at Kandahar Province and tried to find out how many people were on the ground for Shah Wali Kot, I saw nothing. I mean, Shah Wali Kot was not even on the list. I started to wonder, where am I going? By the second week, I received a short email from the Kandahar Chief of Staff welcoming me to Kandahar Province. Many people were copied in the email. I replied to everyone on the email and asked if they could send me some information from Shah Wali Kot since I was assigned there. Not surprisingly, I received emails telling me that there is no civilian diplomatic Chief of Mission presence in Shah Wali Kot. Chief of Mission means diplomats who head a diplomatic mission. So I began to ask where I was supposed to go. I received an email from one of the U.S. Embassy representatives telling me that, for the moment, I was not assigned to go to Shah Wali Kot. So there remained the big question: Where was I going? As I already mentioned, working in this environment, you have to be ready for the unknown and you have to learn to improvise. It was good to break the ice with the email exchange as I wanted to find out where I was going. I was told I was going for sure to Kandahar Province, as I was part of the big civilian surge there.

An interesting anecdote happened to me with regards to my assignment. This happened on the last day of the training, and we had an interesting "speaker." I will call the speaker Robert. Robert had the last spot in the afternoon and everyone was tired and ready to end the training. I was particularly interested to hear from this individual because he just completed his tour in Kandahar Province at a DST. I was still confused on what a DST was and the trainers were not clear with the explanation. In essence, the DST was a smaller version of a PRT. When Robert came, he began to talk about his experience in the District of Maiwand. His speech lasted only 30 minutes but those 30 minutes left everyone with the impression that working in the field in Afghanistan was horrible. Robert told us that he hadn't had a good experience working with the military and the Afghans. He said that living conditions at the DST were extremely bad. I was quite surprised by how much negativity came out of his mouth. He painted Maiwand as a district where nobody would want to go. Rather than motivating me, his speech was discouraging. I said to myself, "boy, that's a district where I don't want to go!" When he ended his speech, nobody wanted to talk to him. He looked arrogant and gave the impression of not having good people skills. I told one of the guys who was sitting at my table, I am not surprised that he didn't get along with the military or Afghans. He doesn't seem to send good vibes and is very arrogant. I told myself that it is what it is. I am not going to dwell on someone's negative experience.

    A couple of weeks later after Robert's talk I found out where I was going. As you have probably guessed, it was Maiwand! This is something that I will address in the next section of the book. When the class ended, we had two days to get ready to go to a civilian-military training exercise. This exercise was the last phase of the training before going to Afghanistan. The training took place in a Training Center. The objective was to teach us what to expect while living on the front lines. When you live and work on the front lines you could expect insurgent attacks. The trainers wanted us to be prepared to take care of ourselves. Although the training was challenging, I think it was pretty effective because they developed realistic scenarios with real Afghans. I remember we had a small scenario where I played the lead role of a PRT meeting with an Afghan Provincial Governor. The meeting was more of a meet-

and-greet, with Afghans telling you their problems and requesting solutions. I did a good job engaging with the Provincial Governor. After we completed the exercise, the Afghan who played the Provincial Governor asked me if I had done this type of work before. I told him that I had prior experience working with locals in developing countries. He told me that I would do well in Afghanistan. The trainers tried to make the scenario as realistic as possible. Each group had the opportunity to reflect on lessons learned, which I think was important. By the time the training ended, I was already tired of it and ready to start working.

When I left the Training Center, I only had two days to spend with my sister and then it was time to depart to Afghanistan. The flight was going to be long. I left from Dulles Airport and flew direct to Dubai. The duration of the flight was over 13 hours. Then I had a layover in Dubai and flew the next day to Kabul. The flight from Dubai to Kabul wasn't that long, around two hours.

III

ON THE BRINK

It was the last week of January when I arrived in Kabul, Afghanistan. As we landed there, through the window I saw the Kabul Mountains. It was late afternoon and sunny. I had searched a bit for YouTube videos of Kabul International Airport. From the videos, Kabul Airport looked small, and it was indeed small. As we began to descend I was a bit nervous because I was landing in one of the most dangerous countries in the world. It was cold and sunny. We arrived on a Sunday. There was no going back and no regrets. I had to move forward and it was time to begin thinking about how I was going to survive one long year. When we landed, everything was chaotic and disorganized. I traveled with the folks I met when I reported to the State Department and we all lined up outside the terminal and waited for the U.S. Embassy staff to pick us up. I was surprised at the flow of people coming in and out. It didn't look as there was strong security. We waited for about 30 minutes before a representative from the U.S. Embassy came to greet us. He had a roll call list and called our names, then we were told to get our bags and walk to the cars. We kept a very low profile. We drove during what appeared to be rush hour. People looked at me weird and I saw women wearing Burqas, an outer garment that women wear in public to cover their bodies. It is part of their Islamic religion. I refrained from taking pictures. I didn't want to bring too much attention to myself. I guess it is common for locals to see many foreigners use the roads that come in and out from Kabul International Airport.

The Embassy staff greeted us and told us to drop our bags on the floor so the dogs could smell the bags for bombs. Then they gave us Afghan cell phones. Accommodations were limited, so they put many of us in one room with six people in it. We had bunk beds and had to adjust, but were very tired from the flight and wanted to at least have some rest. I was still wondering where I was going to go. We were provided with an agenda for the next five days and were required to stay at the Embassy and go through in process training. Yes, more training and paperwork. Actually, I think this training was really a waste of time because it didn't add much substance. A lot of the stuff was just redundant. We spent majority of the time learning how USAID works. Then the other part of the training was on how to fix a car? Well, for those who could self-drive in the north of Afghanistan, this training was probably useful because if something happens to you on the road, you should be prepared to fix it or know the basics. For those of us that were going to a DST and were going to be in a military base, there was no need to go through this training. Then we had the usual in-process paperwork.

Finally, after days of more training and paperwork, I was told that I was going to go to Kandahar Air Field (KAF). From there, I would find out my assignment. I was ready to leave the Embassy; Kabul in the wintertime is not that great. The weather is pretty cold, and it snows. I was ready to go. We woke up early and departed to an airfield, which was located close to the airport. The flight to Kandahar was about an hour and a half. The view from Kabul was fantastic, with mountains covered with snow. We landed in the early afternoon in KAF. We were late so we were not sure if someone was going to greet us. As I was leaving the plane, I only saw a big open space and heard a lot of noise. There was an SUV with two people in it. They were taking someone to the plane. My colleague and I were staring at each other and asked each other, so now who do we contact? Those two folks that we saw on an SUV dropping off somebody asked me who I was. I told them that we were new State Department personnel in Afghanistan and were in KAF to report to the Kandahar Team (KT). The KT supported the DSTs in Kandahar Province. Representatives from several U.S. government agencies such as the State Department and USAID composed the DSTs. The DSTs varied in size, depending on how large the FOB, or COP was. The two people from the SUV took us to Area A. Area A was sort of like our central policy office base for all Regional South Afghanistan. It also supported the DSTs. Because we are still at war and these stories will be available to the public, I will not go into details to describe Area A. KAF is very big and it could be its own city in itself. It houses all Regional South coalitions' forces. Aside from housing the coalition forces, it also hosts multiple contractors. Contractors are everywhere and you could easily identify them. KAF has probably everything you need to make your tour in Afghanistan comfortable. It has several large cafeterias, military post exchanges (PX), gyms, coffee shops, retailers, and fast food restaurants. The military PX's are retail stores. You could find many things in a PX such as movies, food, magazines, and electronics. For instance, there was an American and a German PX in KAF. KAF is a city in itself and living there is like living in a bubble. It is not the real Afghanistan. In KAF you didn't interact with Afghans, only with expats. After spending a few hours in KAF, I would have preferred to live in a DST. I was happy to know that I wasn't going to live in KAF because I didn't know how useful I would be since I would not be working side by side with Afghans.

When I arrived to Area A, there was no room for us to host my colleague and me. I am not kidding, there were no preparations and people were not really expecting us. We were dropped there like lost luggage. They put my colleague and I in a small room. He slept on a flat mattress on the floor and I slept on a military cot. A military cot is like a Nylon bed. I knew that I wasn't going to spend that much time in KAF so it didn't really bother me much. We didn't have a Director in Area A and I tried to speak with folks on the current governance situation in Kandahar Province but I didn't get much information. In a way, it think it was useful that I started to read about Afghanistan before my training in Washington, DC because I knew there was a possibility that I wasn't going to receive any assistance from the folks on the ground. Finally, the KT told the folks in Area A that it was time for my colleague and I to come to the KT. Even then, I still had no idea where I was going to go. My colleague was under the impression that he was going to go to the border with Pakistan, but his assignment was changed as soon as we arrived at the KT. So I left Area A, without any useful knowledge. My colleague and I left on a ground convoy with the Canadians. Back then, there were continuous ground convoys from KAF to KT. The ground convoy didn't last long. It was probably only a 35 minute ride. Kandahar City was not that far from KAF. We arrived late afternoon and the KT DST coordinator greeted us. My colleague and I were again roommates. Actually, it was that late evening when it was decided where I was going to go. The DST coordinator introduced me to the KT Chief of Staff. He was very nice and was relatively new to Afghanistan. After, I met with him we met with the KT Director. It was already late evening when I finally found out where I was going to go. I was assigned to the District of Maiwand. When he said Maiwand I thought about Robert who came to our training class and told us of his experiences there. You see now why I will never forget this anecdote. The KT Director spoke about the Maiwand District Governor (DG) Mr. Karimi. The KT Director described a bad governance and development situation. Prior to the meeting with the KT Director, the DST coordinator asked me how much experience I had working with the military. I told him that I had good experience working with the military in Iraq. The DST coordinator only told me that it is good that I have experience with the military and that I was the right person for this assignment. I didn't know what he meant then, as he didn't go into details. I came to realize what he meant when I began to speak with the KT Director. When Robert came to talk to us in our class, he told us that he didn't have a good relationship with the military. He gave the impression that it was the military's fault that governance and development in Maiwand wasn't moving forward. The KT Director told me that, to the contrary, it was Robert who had a difficult time developing a governance and development strategy that could put Maiwand on track. I wasn't surprised what the KT Director told me as I knew and got the impression that Robert was excusing himself from something that he probably knew was his fault. Maiwand district was on the brink of collapse. The DST wasn't implementing a project. I was told the civilian–military relationship was not good, to the point that the commanding officer for the area of operations (the BSO) got into a heated argument with Robert, who was the lead for the DST. The DST didn't have a good relationship with the District Governor and other key Afghan officials. There wasn't a good link and communication between the Afghan Provincial Government and the District Government. There wasn't a clear direction and mentorship with the Afghan counterparts where they can learn how to be self-sustaining. Good mentorship to our Afghan counterparts was a key factor to our success in order for them to be accountable to their community; however, it appeared that the mentorship was an important element that was missing.

Everything appeared to be stalled and there was a need for someone with experience to mitigate the inter-personal relationships. I was told DG Karimi didn't have a good reputation for being credible and there was a strong possibility he would be replaced. I told the KT Director that I would see what I could do and that I was going to Maiwand with low expectations. It is always important to lower your expectations in this type of work. If you come to the front lines with high expectations, you could find yourself with another reality and at the end you would get frustrated very easily. If you go with low expectations, you would be able to manage your resources better and focus on realistic outputs. I told them that I wanted to go to the district and make my own judgment. Based on lessons learned, I knew that sometimes what is written in intelligence reports might not really represent the true reality. But again, I was put in a tough situation to turn something around that in the beginning appeared unthinkable. Putting myself in challenging situations wasn't something new for me. These situations have increased my confidence and pushed myself to be able to do the unthinkable. I had some fear going to Maiwand. You didn't want to act like you are superhero and that you would change everything right away. You have to accept true feelings like fear. It is normal having fear when you are about to take a tough assignment. Maybe we didn't want to show it to those who surround us. When you have these feelings, it is important to be wise and know how to use these feelings to your advantage. Make the feelings positive! I used fear to my advantage. Fear allowed me to search for inspiration and positive action, and find positive lights within the darkest cloud. Fear was a sense of motivation, which demonstrated how far my leadership capability had gone.

After my meeting, I was told that it was important for me to depart as soon as possible. Finally, I was given the go ahead that I would leave the next day, sometime in the morning. A special military flight came to pick me up on a cloudy and rainy day. I was told the flight would not last too long, maybe 15 minutes. The only person who I knew was going to receive me was a DST colleague (who I will call Michael) who was assigned to the DST in Maiwand. If I am not mistaken it was a Monday when I arrived in there. From the air, the COP looked very small compared to the large bases I was used to in Iraq. As soon as I landed, I got out of the helicopter and walked towards an open area. As the helicopter began to rise up again, I saw my colleague. Michael came up to me, asked me for my name, and welcomed me to Maiwand. He was very nice and took me to my temporary housing. I stayed in a temporary trailer, which was used by the U.S. Special Forces. There was a lot of water around where our DST was located. I arrived to Maiwand during rainy season, so I was told to be ready to get wet.

My colleague told me that my other colleague (who I will call Scramble) was at a Shura with DG Karimi and elders. A Shura is an informal meeting where Afghans get together to discuss their problems. A Shura could be short but most of the time they are long. As you read more of my stories, I will discuss the Shuras and how they could be effective or just a waste of time. The DST became a team of three but only for a few days. Michael was already scheduled to leave for another district, and I was about to take his trailer. Scramble was getting ready to go on R&R in a week and a half and there was a bit of pressure for me to get up to speed right away. I was going to be left alone soon to run an operation without really overlapping with the folks who had been on the ground and could teach me about the district. I didn't want these situations to come up because they add more difficulty to the adjustment. But I had to deal with it.

When I went to my temporary trailer, I began to think about what I had gotten myself into. It is normal to second-guess the decisions you make when you come to work in this environment, especially on the front lines. Michael briefly took me around the COP and showed me where the facilities were located. I was coming from Iraq where I lived on a large base, with reasonable living trailers, a gym, and cafeterias. Here, it was a complete turnaround. There were no real bathrooms. We had a shower, gym, and a cafeteria tent. As we walked around, Michael introduced me to some military colleagues, and I got a cold greeting. In the back of my mind, I knew that because Robert who worked in Maiwand left on bad terms, there was probably a feeling that I was going to be the same as him. I began to think that it would be important to build trust amongst my future colleagues. The COP was run by a U.S. Army infantry brigade composed of several platoons, commanded by a Captain. I think we had around 200 soldiers. Michael and I ate at the cafeteria tent and the food was not the typical of a large Forward Operating Base (FOB). In large FOBs you will have a larger menu and have the flexibility to pick from a variety range of food. While at the COP you didn't have that option. We had a field kitchen and you ate whatever they served you. I didn't have an issue because it was about adjustment. After we had lunch, I went back to my temporary trailer and Michael told me to wait for Scramble, so we could all meet as a team. I wanted to discuss the governance and development efforts, and Michael told me that nothing had been done in Maiwand regarding governance and development. To the contrary there were a lot of burned bridges that needed to be repaired. When Scramble came to the trailer I asked if there were reports from Maiwand on governance and development that I could read to get familiarized with the situation, but there were none. It was important for me to not try to do something that had already been done or tried without success. For me, it was important to not waste time on resources. Both Michael and Scramble told me that there was nothing written on Maiwand. I was quite shocked when I heard this and asked them why. I thought it was important to have something written on the district so when visitors came they had something to read about it. Then both Michael and Scramble began to tell me the struggles with Robert. Yes, I have to go back to Robert again because he was the previous team leader for the DST. I asked Michael and Scramble who the current DST team leader was, but there wasn't one. They told me the military would soon identify the next one. (From now on when I refer to the "military" I am referring to my military counterparts who lived in the COP and who were my partners in governance and development.) Michael and Scramble informed me that no mentorship existed to DG Karimi. I asked them what their impression was of him and I didn't get good feedback. They told me he was lazy and didn't seem to be engaged with the community's needs. They told me that he gives the impression that he doesn't know what he is doing, confirming reports I read before arriving that said many Afghan government officials assume a position but didn't really know how to execute. It is always important to listen to other people's opinions. I knew at one point I was going to have my own judgment on how the DG performed and I would test his knowledge on government issues. They also told me that the DG seemed friendly but needed mentorship. I asked if there was a District Development Assembly (DDA). There was none. I asked how many people we had working in the District Government. I didn't get a number count. I asked them how were the communication between the Line Ministry Directors in Kandahar City with the District Government. I was told that there was none. I asked how many USAID projects have been implemented in Maiwand. There were very few. There was one USAID implementing partner located in the COP and I was told that he was someone that I should meet because he engaged with DG Karimi and the community. I would call this person Virginia. I asked very basic questions related to governance and development. Going back to what I said regarding the importance of doing your own research proved accurate. The question that I asked about the existence of a DDA was something that I wasn't taught during the training. I came to Maiwand with a broad picture on what I could expect to see at the district level, basically how dysfunctional it could be. I am glad I read a large number of reports because some of the information that I read reflected what I was hearing from Michael and Scramble. So in a way, I was already ahead of the game in terms of putting my ideas and vision to work on how to move forward with my work in Maiwand. There wasn't going to be another Shura for the next four days or so, so that gave me some time to begin to speak to people in the COP and prepare myself before I introduced myself to DG Karimi.

I went back to my trailer and looked again at the reports that I had saved and researched prior to the start of my training. As I went through them, I began to picture the current governance situation. One of the first things that struck me was that there wasn't anything written on the district. When I was in Iraq, I was confronted with a similar situation. I was never handed a governance report that provided me with key data and the governance outlook. So I did something similar to what I did in Iraq: I began to develop an outline on topics that would be important to have in a governance report. I also included whatever development initiatives had been completed. For governance, it was important to highlight the government structure, key players' names, and provide a general outlook on the governance situation. I also began to think of a tool that would assist me in monitoring the governance situation, such as the World Bank governance dimensions. All of these tools and initiatives I've mentioned required a lot of homework but I knew the document would assist me with my critical thinking. For the next few days, I would sit in my temporary trailer thinking about how to prepare for my first Shura.

Scramble introduced me to the USAID implementer partner representative Virginia, who implemented small community grant projects. For example, Virginia provided assistance to the school located next to our base. I sat with Virginia and asked him about his impression of DG Karimi. Virginia told me that DG Karimi was probably corrupt and didn't seem to care about Maiwand, and that it was probably time for him to go. Virginia was probably the only person at that moment at the COP that provided me with a breakdown of the key players in Maiwand, including pictures and names. After I spoke to Virginia, I knew it was time to speak with my military counterparts. Working with the military was going to be a huge task because of the previous problems with Robert. We had a new Commanding Officer (CO) because the previous CO was injured. When I met the CO, he gave me a cold greeting. The CO was a young Captain and I was told he was very busy. He was the CO for the COP. I didn't have a problem and was always respectful and professional. We had a very small military team (I would call it Team D) that was assigned to support the DST on governance and development. Michael and Scramble introduced me to the Team D members and they were very distant. I asked Michael and Scramble why I got such a cold reception and they told me that Team D was upset at Robert and they probably had the impression that I was going to be just like him. I was told that I still had to meet the Battle Space Owner (BSO), the high-ranking commanding officer in charge of the area of operations who was located in another base. Michael and Scramble told me that it was important to engage with the BSO as he was also upset with Robert. It seemed like Robert burned all his bridges with the military. By the end of the day I wasn't feeling well. I wasn't sure if I wanted to be in this position. Everything seemed so negative and I didn't even go outside the COP yet to meet with my real key strategic partner - the District Governor. I didn't know if I was going to have the energy to change something that appeared so broken inside the COP. There was low morale, which impacted creativity and productivity. The military unit living at the COP was getting ready to leave Afghanistan in less than 3 months and their minds were already back home while at the DST we had another year to make it worth. I couldn't walk outside the COP to reflect like what I would do back home if I am frustrated. In my situation I had to suck it up and adjust to the situation. I lied down on my bed and tried to relax and thought that things are going to be fine despite the fact that I didn't feel welcome at all.

Every time I had the opportunity to have some time alone and to reflect, I thought about how I was going to help a district that appeared to be in disrepair. It is important to always play it low key and respect people's opinions instead of jumping in right away. You never want to send the impression that you know better than everyone else and, most importantly, you don't want to do projects and provide ideas without really knowing the real situation. The nerd that I am, I did a small SWOT (Strength, Weaknesses, Opportunity, and Threat) analysis to define my goals and objectives. This is important if you want to excel in the field. My goal was to repair all bridges and put in place a strategic objective where the District Governor can be accountable to the community and establish a strong relationship with the Afghan Provincial

Government. My strength my motivation, weakness the low morale among all key strategic partners, opportunity a new guy is in town meaning "me" and I can repair the broken bridges and bring funding to the district, and threat the rise of the insurgent activity on the Spring. The Taliban strongest campaign is on the Spring and Summer.

It was a Monday when I got ready to go to my first Shura and my colleague Scramble was going to introduce me to DG Karimi. It was a Security Shura, where the security heads and military speak on their joint operations. Nothing about development was discussed. I still attended the Shura to engage with DG Karimi. We linked up with the military right by our gate and Team D provided us with the escort. Each time we went out the gate we had to be escorted by the military. I met our BSO during the link-up with the military. He had a smile on his face and he welcomed me to Maiwand. I introduced myself as the Department of State representative who has been assigned to Maiwand to work on governance. Once we concluded the brief introduction, we all got ready to go to the District Center. Scramble came with me to the Shura. Scramble was in charge of development and would stay with me for almost my entire tour. Since Robert left, Scramble was told to do the governance work as well until I arrived. Michael stayed behind, as he was getting ready to go to another district.

So we all walked outside the COP on our way to the District Center where I would meet DG Karimi for the first time. As we took the short walk, Scramble was telling me about the development projects that had been done in Maiwand. We walked by a school right outside the COP and Scramble told me that the school received USAID assistance. We continued to walk straight to an open area. To my right side there was a busy bazaar. In front of me, a dried river. The District Center was on my left. Right by the river, every Monday and Thursday, villagers got together to trade their sheep, so it could get very congested. Many Afghans drove motorcycles, often with two people riding. The woman is always in the back seat. When we got to the end of the road we made a left towards the District Center, where people stopped to stare at us. Locals could tell when someone is new and they were curious about who I was. Some locals thought I was an Afghan because of my facial looks because I can pass as a northern Afghan. If you are an Afghan working for the Americans, some locals may think of you as a traitor. But as soon as the locals heard me speaking in English and found out my name they knew I wasn't an Afghan. The main entrance block for the District Center had T-walls, large concrete walls used for blast protection. On the side of the walls, I saw people sitting on the ground waiting to go inside to request or get approval for their Afghan Identification Cards (also known as Tashkeras). I also saw women and they were all covered with Burqas, sitting in a corner separate from the men. The Afghan National Police (ANP) guarded the District Center. Once I got in, it was an open area with many buildings. The District Center is a large compound that was built to house the DG and government civil servant workers. To my left, I saw people waiting outside the Taskhera building. There was a Mosque inside the District Center, but there wasn't much activity among the government civil servants workers. On the back of the District Center, the ANP had its headquarters and behind it there was an Agriculture Center with six buildings that were not being utilized.

After quickly observing the structure of the District Center, it was time to meet the person that I was going to work with and make sure he would lead the district. At that point, I didn't know how long I was going to work with DG Karimi, as there was a rumor that he may be removed. I didn't let that bother me and went forward. Like I've told my colleagues before I came to Maiwand, it is important I make one's own judgment about the DG and see what he could do. People have different styles. Scramble introduced me to DG Karimi and he welcomed me to the District Center. He was about my same height and more overweight. He had a cigarette on his hand and when he smoked he will smile at you. He appeared quiet and reserved, clearly skeptical about what my intentions were for the district. He presented himself like he was somebody who didn't know much about the functionality of a district government. Later on I would find out that he was extremely smart about local politics, and I learned from him as he learned from me. DG Karimi tested me many times on how much I knew about the Afghan government functionality and every time I passed his tests. The introduction was very short because he had to speak with the other security heads that attended the Security Shura to discuss the ongoing joint operations. I had a feeling that DG Karimi was probably skeptical about me because of Robert. I knew I had to demonstrate to him that I could turnaround the district. This would prove to be a great challenge and I would discuss later how we put the district back on track.

When DG Karimi began the Shura he introduced me to the security heads. I thanked DG Karimi for the introduction. I stood up and introduced myself. When you stand up and talk, it demonstrates a lot of respect to the Afghans and they really appreciate it. It was quite a feeling standing up and looking in everyone's eyes. In their eyes, they were probably thinking, Who is this guy? Can he deliver? Would he be the same as the others who do a lot of talk and never come through? I saw a low of skepticism through their eyes. It is normal to get this look when you arrive to a new place. As I already mentioned, it would be up to me to demonstrate to DG Karimi and everyone else that we can do something in Maiwand and we can all see the light at the end of the tunnel.

After the Security Shura, I asked DG Karimi if he could come to the COP so we could talk and get to know each other. It was important to establish an informal relationship with him; I knew that if our relationship was going to be formal, it would make things more difficult. In many developing countries like Afghanistan, things didn't get accomplished formally. I developed informal relationships with government officials in Eastern Europe and the Middle East. It worked well to my advantage and I wanted to do the same with DG Karimi.

DG Karimi accepted my invitation to come to the COP and talk. On the way back from the District Center to the COP, I told Team D that we were going to meet with DG Karimi. At that time, the Team D leader was still on R&R, and the members who were present looked at me as if they had no confidence that I could do much. So you could see how I was challenged from different fronts and I had to do something to begin to rebuild bridges.

When I came back to the COP, I asked my team members if we had an interpreter. We didn't. When I worked in Iraq, I had dedicated translators working for me. Now, I didn't have one and it would be a challenge to figure out who was going to help the DST translate. It was difficult but I just had to adjust. I asked the Psychological Operations (PSYOPS) team if they could help me with the translation and they provided me with their translator, but he didn't want to help us because he wasn't assigned to the DST. A PSYOPS team is in charge of putting radio messages in the local community and they also provide humanitarian outreach assistance. The translator was an Afghan-American who later became a good friend of mine. Before the meeting, I prepared some notes so I could be ready to meet DG Karimi. I asked my colleagues Michael and Scramble if they were going to join me, but only Scramble did because Michael was pretty much on his way out. In my notes, I had several questions for DG Karimi, such as:

- How did he view the Afghan Government?
- How much support had he received from the Afghan government?
- How much money had he received for development projects?
- What were his priorities?

- How effective were his Tashkiel (or government civil servants)?
- Was there a DDA?
- How did he like his job?
- What kind of assistance was he looking to receive from us?
- How is the security in Maiwand?
- Did he engage with the Provincial Line Ministry Directors?
- Did he attend the Provincial Development Council meeting that are organized monthly?
- What was his relationship with the Provincial Governor (PG)?
- Does he know his roles and responsibilities?
- What had been the challenges since he became a District Governor?

I wrote many questions but I knew he wasn't going to answer all of them. I planned on introducing myself, explaining my role in Maiwand and what possible resources I could bring, and how we could mentor each other. The meeting was a bit formal because we still didn't know each other. He gave me the impression that he didn't know much about how the Afghan government was supposed to support him and how the coalition worked, how USAID or the Embassy worked, or the type of support he is supposed to receive from the Provincial Governor (PG) and Provincial Line Ministry Directors. I told DG Karimi that I realized one of the main problems is how the money gets downstream from Kabul to the Districts. The aid sometimes gets stuck somewhere in between Kabul and the Provincial Capital. He told me that he was aware of this problem. When I asked him how many people he had working for him, he told me nobody and that he did everything himself. I would find out later that he had 9 Afghan Tashkiel workers that work for him. He also mentioned that he didn't have a budget and that he didn't know how USAID worked. One of the first things I learned is that it would take weeks for me to gain DG Karimi's trust and once he opened himself up to me, it would be much easier to move forward with the governance and development efforts. What I found interesting from the meeting is that there was no leader from our side. Scramble told me to take the lead on the meeting as Team D didn't want to. This responsibility was put on me right away and I had to improvise. Sudden challenges such as this have made me a stronger leader. I was put on the spot and it was up to me to figure out right away how to lead a team that is on the brink of collapse, with no motivation. One of my priorities was to keep the meeting positive and to send a message to everyone, including DG Karimi, that it was not over yet in Maiwand and that we could still turn it around.

One of the first thing I learned is that it will take weeks for me to gain DG Karimi's trust and once he opened himself to me, it made a lot things easier in order for us to move forward with the governance and development efforts. DG Karimi and I developed a good working relationship and I demonstrated to him that I could deliver. I didn't promise much which help to keep the pressure off in an environment where a lot of things are expected from you to accomplish. But what I promised to him that I will do I delivered and that was my goal to success in Maiwand. I not only earned the respect from DG Karimi but from other key Afghan government officials in Maiwand and the rest of the community.

After the meeting we walked DG Karimi to the gate. I asked Team D and Scramble about their impression of the meeting. I didn't get a positive or negative answer; it was basically indifference and lack of faith that anything could be done. I went back to my trailer and spoke quickly to Michael and Scramble. They both told me that it would be difficult to make something happen in this district. The negativity from both Michael and Scramble didn't help me much. I didn't want to be discouraged. Actually, if I went by everyone's feeling of negativity, I could have just tagged along and confirmed to my superiors that we couldn't make it happen in Maiwand. I could have just written weekly reports and that would have been my only task in Afghanistan. But I didn't want that to happen. Deep inside of my heart I knew there was good in DG

Karimi and that we could turn Maiwand around. I knew that we could change the low morale of the DST, military, and Afghan counterparts. I went back to my trailer and I kept scratching my head about how I was going to turnaround Maiwand. What kind of projects could I provide to the district? I knew I had to deliver something, because in this environment talk was cheap. I'd been doing this work for so many years that I had learned my own lessons. Below are some of the mistakes practitioners make when they come to the field in a war zone:

- They come motivated to the field and in the first three months they promise to assist everyone.
- After the fourth month, locals begin to ask for those promises.
- By the fifth month, they get frustrated because they have realized that it is difficult to deliver something.
- By the sixth month, they have lost full credibility with the locals and people will not ask for things. If they do, they will do it to see if whether you can still do something but they will not have expectations.
- By the seventh month, they haven't delivered something and begin to withdraw from the local engagement.
- After that, they will find themselves on another assignment. If you extend for another year and you are still talking without some substance, then they should not be working in the field.

It is important not to lose credibility by making promises you can't keep. Here is what I would recommend, and what I've done:

- Start low key.
- Listen to the local problems.
- Do your homework and research. Don't be lazy because, in the field, nothing is going to be delivered to you on a golden plate. If it happens, great. But critical thinking is important because it would allow you to think about deliverables and resources. Look for possible funds that

might exist and are at your disposal. Some of these funds are never used.
- Don't take credit for others' effort. If the military has Commanders Emergency Response Program (CERP) funds, then mentor and assist your military counterparts on where or how to spend development funds. However, you would not have complete management and ownership of the project. In the end, the military would do whatever they want with their funds and you have to respect that.
- When you meet with the locals, expect a lot of requests. Don't promise anything.
- Be honest about what you could possibly deliver. Locals appreciate honesty and straightforwardness.
- Try to do small projects first and measure the impact.
- The more small projects you could do, the better you would feel about the level of impact. It would also keep you busy. If you focus on one large project that requires a substantial amount, and you didn't have a large staff to support you, you could waste a lot of time.

Scramble told me that he would be leaving soon on vacation and I would have to lead the team. As I mentioned, nothing on Maiwand was written down, so I had to develop a governance report. I like doing these types of reports. The governance report had key generic information on the structure and demographics of the district, plus pictures of government authorities, biographical information, and development information. Doing this really helped me because two weeks later I was instructed to provide a governance and development presentation to the KT on Maiwand. No kidding, I was tasked to present and talk about the district less than three weeks after my arrival. I didn't mind doing it but I didn't know how effective an opinion I could provide given that I was new in the district and still getting to know the key players and government environment. Every night until the end of my tour, I kept going back to the governance report. The governance report became the bible of all my knowledge and it gave visitors a glance at the district's direction. I forecasted how the district was moving forward.

On my second week, we had a People's Shura. During the International Security Assistance Force (ISAF) and Afghan National Security Forces (ANSF) joint operations there were arrests, and at the People's Shura elders came to the district and spoke on detainee cases. I went to the People' Shura and observed how the elders complained and vouched for their relatives. It was chaotic and we had a lot of elders, probably around 60, in one medium-sized conference room. Many detainees were detained because they were caught with drugs or were involved in an insurgent activity. The elders vouched for their relatives by telling the ANSF and ISAF that their relatives would not commit the act they were caught for again. We didn't have a judge or an attorney general to prosecute cases; so many times the detainees would remain in jail for a short period of time, and then get released. The elders brought pictures of their relatives and some had been coming to the People's Shura vouching for a relative who had been detained several months prior with no information on the whereabouts. It was sad to see it because some elders would cry, asking for their relatives, but no information could be provided because the relative could get lost in the system and there was no track record. So the District Governor had to intervene and mediate the elders' request to the ANSF and ISAF. DG Karimi didn't introduce me to the elders because he knew that my focus wasn't security. The Development Shura was the important Shura for us at the DST because it dealt with all good governance and reconstruction development projects. At the Security and People's Shura I sat towards the end of the table but still was relatively close to the all the key players such as the District Governor, Afghan Security Heads and ISAF military counterparts. To the contrary, at the Development Shura, I sat next to the District Governor. I was happy that on my first week I didn't have a Development Shura because it allowed me to continue to research what kind of funds I may have available to bring to Maiwand. I went back to my Iraq experience and wanted to find out if the funds that I had available for development programs were also available in Afghanistan. I found out that I had similar funds available in Afghanistan. So I began with the process of registering to the funding operating system. Once registered, I went inside the website to look at the types of development programs that Embassy funded. The grants are small but it varies by the type of program such as education, community activities, media, etc. I noticed that not much funding had been utilized. Comparing the amounts that were used in Iraq, the funding appropriated in Afghanistan was really small. The majority of the grants were provided to large PRTs and not much to the DST. So I knew that if I could make this happen and bring these funds to the DST, it would be an accomplishment and a big success for the DST in Maiwand. I began to contact the folks at the Embassy in charge of this program and I asked them questions about, among other things, how long the approval process was. I didn't go into detail explaining to them what kind of projects we had planned because I was still getting to know my district, but I wanted to get a general idea. You see, a lot of the stuff that I am explaining is like doing homework and research: It takes time and preparation. Being prepared is important. I knew at my first Development Shura people were going to ask me for a lot of things. I knew it would be easy for me to say "I would see what I could do," since I was new. But I knew that I couldn't say this all the time because at some point the locals would look for results.

From Thursday to Sunday it got slow. Friday is the day of rest for Afghans, so Afghan government officials only had to work from Saturday through Thursday. The District Center functioned from Sunday through Wednesday afternoon. It was uncommon to see Afghans coming to the District Center on a Thursday. As the weeks passed, I found myself working on the weekends, sometimes alongside my Afghan counterparts. Michael left on a Saturday and I took over his trailer. I was moving around for two months and I was looking forward to settling in to the trailer and making it feel like home. It didn't have a bathroom like my trailer in Iraq, but the inside was nice because it had plastic wood, which gave it a different feeling. There are trailers that are plain gray on the inside and it's just depressing. Okay, I may be exaggerating, but for some reason the color of plastic wood made it comfortable. I worked and lived in my trailer. I had a small refrigerator, twin bed, and my workspace. It was very simple and nothing special. One thing that was nice was that I had Internet and a direct phone, from which I could call the states. It was convenient not to have to go to the MWR in the COP. The MWR is the Army Moral, Welfare, and Recreation room that provides leisure services to the soldiers in the COP.

Scramble told me that he was leaving soon and that I would be on my own for an entire month. We got about 60 days or so of leave and we got to decide how we wanted to break down our leave, either split them into three Rest and Recuperations (R&Rs), where you could be out of the country for three times a year, or two R&Rs and three Regional Rest Breaks. I went with the option of three R&Rs a year and so did my colleague. Scramble's R&R in February was his first R&R and he was definitely looking forward to it. We only had one more week to work together, then I would not see him until the end of February or early March. Because we lived in a small COP, military flights didn't come very often and you had to go to another base, overnight at a transit tent, then go on Space A (aka standby) and try to get a seat on a military or contractor's helicopter. At that time, the U.S. Embassy Air asset still didn't come to our COP, so you had to leave at least a week earlier or more to give yourself the time to find a way out of Maiwand. It was the same ordeal coming back. You had to find a way to return either by ground convoy, military, or contractor helicopter. But it wasn't going to be easy to come to the COP Rath. "Rath" was the name of the COP. Later on it would change to COP Hutal. Afghans call the District Center of Maiwand "Hutal." Hutal is the main center of Maiwand where the District Center,

Bazaar, COP Rath, and main school were located. I call COP Rath or COP Hutal just COP.

On the weekend, I met with Team D and Scramble to discuss what we were going to do. At that time the Team D leader came back from R&R. I will call Team D Leader "Hawaii." Hawaii was skeptical about what I was going to do. I received a cold greeting from him. At that time, I didn't know that he also had had a terrible relationship with Robert. One of the first things I wanted to do that I felt wasn't done properly was to make the team engagement inclusive, empower all key players, and keep them informed about everything that was going on. In this environment you couldn't think that you could do everything on your own; you need people to support you, even if you didn't need them to do any work. When you are frustrated, you need somebody to laugh with or talk to. It was important to be friendly and professional. Information was not provided sufficiently to Team D's and they didn't have a clear idea of how the DST really functioned or what the role and expectations were from the State Department and USAID. So I began to send Team D information regarding how we work, and I forwarded them the documents or emails that I had received from KT or Area A. I also made myself available to Team D for information on governance and development. Just like we got requests from our higher-ups, Team D got them too, and it was important that I was ready to answer any questions. For instance, sometimes the request would be to know how many people the District Governor has working for him, and whether or not they are effective. So Team D would come to my trailer and ask for my opinion before they sent an answer to the RFI (Request for Information). It wasn't a big deal for me.

I wanted to find out more on how the military had provided humanitarian assistance to the locals. Team D told me that the last Civil Affairs (CA) team member was leaving in three days. The CA team is important because they do community development work. I was a bit concerned that the CA team was leaving the COP because I knew they had resources that could help everyone in Maiwand. Later in the year, we had another CA team, but for half of my tour we didn't have one.

I asked Team D what the timeline was for the military unit that was on the COP to leave Afghanistan and they told me that it was in March, although their work would end in February. Well, that was something else that I had to adjust to. Strategically, I realized that coming to Maiwand before the new military unit arrives in late March, would provide me with more ground time to get to know the area, and the DST would be one of the few continuities for governance and development. So in a way, it was probably good that the current military unit was leaving because it would allow me time to develop a foundation. Team D was also leaving in a couple of weeks. But no matter what, I wanted to fix the civilian-military relationship. It was important to demonstrate that the DST was a team player and wanted to include everybody.

As the days passed by, I continued to sit with Team D to brainstorm governance and development objectives and find a way forward. At the same time, I continued to meet constantly with DG Karimi and my governance report started to become important. When it was time to attend my first Development Shura, I had a basic understanding of what was done in the district and had an idea of what I wanted to do with the available U.S. Embassy funds I had at my disposal. I expected a lot of people to complain that we didn't do much for Maiwand and that they would want more. The USAID implementing partner representative, Virginia, also attended the Development Shura, as he was an important partner for implementing small community projects. The room was crowded. DG Karimi introduced me to the elders as the new member of the DST first, and then I stood up and introduced myself. Following my own recommendation, I didn't promise much. I was more of a listener and told them that I would see what I could do. I wanted to observe how DG Karimi managed the elders' expectations and how the military engaged with the local population on development matters. It is important that you observe first how people around you work and behave. This would give you an advantage on how to proceed. You always want to be cautious about what you say and remember teachable moments. Overall, I think the meeting went well. After the Development Shura, I had elders telling me how much water and electricity they needed. I told them that I understood their problem and I would see what I could do. I never promised anything. When I came back to the COP I told Scramble that it was important that we begin to think how we were going to engage with the people at the Development Shura because we couldn't just be sitting around listening to their problems all year. It was important to engage the Afghan Government officials because, at the end of the day, we would eventually leave and DG Karimi would be left with these problems. As DG Karimi and I began to develop a relationship, I mentored him on the importance of engaging with the Provincial Governor (PG) and the key Line Ministry Directors so they could assist the district. The DST and military could not solve everyone's problems, and it was important for Afghans to take the lead. My meetings with DG Karimi started to become daily and I always included Team D and Scramble. Before I arrived, the members of Team D felt like outsiders. Suddenly, Team D was thanking me for making the outreach effort to help our Afghan counterparts and make the process more inclusive. I began to develop a friendship with DG Karimi. I wanted DG Karimi to think that he had on me a close adviser and a friend that he can count on for all governance and development efforts.

One of the most difficult aspects of my time in Afghanistan was transmitting my message to DG Karimi or other local counterparts. Whenever I had to meet DG Karimi in the COP, I always had to run around the COP trying to find a good translator. I never asked somebody to go and find me a translator because it would send the wrong image; you didn't want to delegate and it was important that you find out your own resources. I asked the

KT for a translator and they told me that I had to figure it out on my own. I had to ask the military to lend me a translator every time I need it to engage with an Afghan counterpart. My military counterparts were often on patrols with the translators. When they came back, the translators were exhausted and the last thing they wanted to do was more translation, especially for me. So it was important to establish a good relationship with my military counterparts and their translators. I always thought strategically and knew the importance of building relationships. With good relationships, I could make things easier.

Scramble was ready to leave and we didn't have a two-week overlap to work together. We had to write the weekly reports like any organization and I noticed our weekly reports were a bit disorganized, so before Scramble left I told him that I would revise the weekly reports and make them more focused. It was important to send a message through our weekly reports that the DST Maiwand is in process of fixing everything, from writing the reports to addressing the governance and development programs. And right before Scramble departed, I was instructed to do a presentation for my higher ups on the governance and development efforts. I said, why not? Actually, I looked on the bright side because I came to realize that this program's direction was mine to decide. I only had seven days to prepare. I said goodbye to Scramble and was running the DST alone. After Scramble left, I went to Team D and asked them if we could work together on the presentation. As I already mentioned, it is important to make people feel included and I wanted to empower my military counterparts. By doing so, they would be inspired to provide ideas or to support you in any way. When I approached Team D to work on the presentation, they were surprised that I reached out to them but were pleased with the team relationship I wanted to build. So we all talked about the structure of the presentation. It included basic information and data on DG Karimi, the geographical, governance and development objectives, and the governance framework for Maiwand. I knew it was important to develop a framework with outputs and inputs because it would keep us all on track. You always want to try to keep things organized. If you lose focus, you could find yourself trying to do many things without a concrete outcome.

The next day I met a new member of the team. He was a U.S. Army Lieutenant Colonel who worked with the Afghans and provided mentorship assistance. I am going to call the new member Hola. That was my nickname for him. When I met Hola, he was also skeptical about me. He also didn't have a good impression of Robert. He was very nice and we bonded very quickly. He was smart and after a couple of days of engagement, he knew I was trying to work things out for the best and rebuild bridges. Hola supported the U.S. Army Special Forces operations and was also embedded in the field to mentor the District Governor. I was impressed with him because he knew how to speak Pashto. Pashto is the language spoken in southern Afghanistan. The U.S. Army does a great job providing language training to their embedded advisors in the field. Hola also knew a bit of Spanish. He was very funny, smart, and after a couple of days of engagement, he knew I was trying to work things out for the best and wanted to help rebuild any bridges that were broken. Hola was smart because he studied well the tribal structure and the connections with the local powerbrokers. I sat many hours with Hola to analyze some of my Afghans counterparts' behavior because some acted according to their tribal affiliation. Hola was also street smart and used a lot of his knowledge to promote my vision for Maiwand. From the military side, both Team D and Hola would become my closest military counterparts for all related governance and development efforts. Finally, once I felt more comfortable talking to Team D and Hola, I asked about Robert. They told me that Robert left a horrible impression on the DST and almost got into a heated argument with the BSO. The BSO was a very nice person and I couldn't imagine that he would instigate a heated argument. Below are several things I am recommending *not* to do:

- Don't act like you know everything,
- Don't tell your military counterparts that you are better than them,
- Don't boss people around,
- Don't promise too much,
- Don't be disrespectful, and
- Don't leave your post every time you have an opportunity. It shows that you aren't committed to your job.

At a meeting with a U.S. Army General, the BSO told me that he was concerned I was going to be like Robert. After three weeks, I began to feel that I was becoming part of the team. The feeling was good and positive. When you get this feeling, you know you are on the right path. I shared the governance report that I was creating with my military counterparts and they liked it. My military counterparts liked the report because it became a tool on the governance and development progress in Maiwand.

In mid-February, it was time to do the presentation for my higher-ups, but unfortunately the poor communications didn't allow me to do it. I sent my power point slides to a military colleague in another base and he read my presentation to the KT. Quite frankly, I didn't know what type of feedback I was going to receive. All I knew was that my military counterparts and I put a lot of effort into it. For the first time in Maiwand, the civilian and military experts were working together. That was a good achievement given how the district was before I landed in Maiwand. In the presentation, I highlighted the joint effort with Team D, the Afghan officials, and the community. It was important to send the message that this DST would be different. I was pleased to receive good feedback from the KT. It was important for the KT to know that we were moving forward in Maiwand.

As the days passed I began to understand better the governance situation in Maiwand. I told Team D and Hola that in order to promote good governance in Maiwand, we would have to mentor DG Karimi on how to exercise his power and make good decisions over time across the spectrum of economic, administrative, and social areas. The objective was to improve the economic and financial management, strengthen law and justice, and increase public sector effectiveness. Good governance in Maiwand meant competent management of the district's resources and affairs in a manner that is open, transparent, accountable, and responsive to the people's needs. We began to have a good relationship with DG Karimi. We were informed that the Kandahar Provincial Governor (PG) was going to visit Maiwand to discuss the governance, reconstruction, and development progress with DG Karimi. I told the Team D and Hola that we could prepare DG Karimi to transmit an effective message. It was important for DG Karimi to send an image of control and leadership. Empowering Afghan officials is a challenge, especially in a rural area like Maiwand, where human capital is at its lowest. Not only was it important to mentor and prepare DG Karimi for the PG's visit, but it was also important for us as a *team* to show that we were changing the governance and development landscape and that progress could be made. As I got to know DG Karimi personally and professionally, I noticed that he was very smart about local politics. He was no fool in terms of how the rules of the game were played at the local level. DG Karimi was also a key powerbroker in Maiwand and he knew a lot of people in Kandahar City. I remember in the first meeting when he told me that he wasn't aware of the budget and what his role was supposed to be in Maiwand. He actually knew a lot more than he let on and I was happy because that made things much easier. He was friendly and we would talk about life and foreign affairs whenever he visited me. He will always have a cigarette on his hand and whenever he smoked he will smile. He really enjoyed smoking his cigarette. When you are talking informally with someone, you know that you are building a good relationship. The person might not be completely open to you, but it's a good step. The fact that I began to build a good relationship already put me in a far better situation.

A District Governor in Afghanistan is appointed. He acts as the enforcer of Afghan policies and manages the district government, but he couldn't really fire or hire people. The system is so centralized that it leaves a DG basically powerless. I knew that but a lot of my team members didn't. Our DG was good with relationships, which made him an influential power broker in the district. However, we lived and worked in a fragile environment surrounded by the Taliban. I liked DG Karimi but I never really knew who he was after I spoke to him. He was always nice to everyone and never really appeared to be surrounded with a lot of security. That brought some questions to me because the Taliban distrusts Afghan officials and when they have an opportunity to kill one, they would do it. Our DG never seemed intimidated by the Taliban. Sometimes in our Shura meetings, he spoke against the Taliban. We all knew that at the Shura meetings there were Taliban spies. It was no surprise and DG Karimi probably knew who they were. I wouldn't have been surprised if DG Karimi communicated with the Taliban in order for him to stay alive, but I didn't know.

When we met as a team with DG Karimi to prepare him with his meeting with the PG, we went over Maiwand's priorities. The priorities were:

    a. Tashkiel – A competent civil servants staff would ensure the efficient delivery of public services.
    b. Economy – The creation of a local factory that would train and employ the local population was essential to decrease the high number of unemployment. Scarcity of water was impacting crop productivity. Farmers needed large storage facilities to store their crops so the crops wouldn't go bad before they reached the local market.
    c. Health – The local clinic needed support with medical supplies and a permanent doctor and nurse.

d. Education – Increasing the number of teachers would facilitate the opening of more schools. Currently 4 (one school is located in the Hutal area, Maslibadab village, Miskari village, and Chismemaran village) out of 15 schools are open.
e. Security – Security improvement was a key component to economic and political development.
f. Roads – Linking more villages with new roads would allow farmers to trade their crops.

As you could see the there were a lot of priorities and the majority were things that needed to be addressed by the Afghan government. Building roads and providing electricity is something that would not be sustainable from donors. This would have to come from the Afghan government because they were required to support public services over the long term. DG Karimi asked me if I could provide the financial support to provide water, electricity, and roads. I was honest with him and told him that we couldn't. I think he knew what my answer was going to be and he didn't pressure with this request throughout the year. As I already mentioned, it was important for him to know what I could realistically provide. DG Karimi told me that he would be ready for the upcoming visit by the PG and we kept meeting on a consistent basis to make sure he kept his points short and clear. Although DG Karimi was smart and knew what he was talking about, it was important for me to make sure he stayed focused, especially if the elders were present at the meeting. When you have a meeting with the elders, sometimes the substance of your conversation could change quickly. The elders didn't listen to structure and because they were so frustrated with the lack of support from the Afghan government, they would talk and continue to make requests for essential services. Not only would they request services but some elders would even make requests for relatives to be released from jail. Once this happens, a meeting' focus can quickly change to security and detainees. We didn't want this to happen for this meeting with the PG. We wanted to keep the focus of this meeting only on governance and reconstruction development.

One of my first big projects in Maiwand was to re-establish the DDA. I knew that if I wanted to do development projects, it was important to have a representative body with a DDA Chairman to assist and coordinate with the development efforts. I learned about the DDA when I was doing my own research about Afghanistan before I started my training. When I began to do my large governance report, I created a government organizational chart and detailed the provincial structure, from the Provincial Governor all the way down to the village level. As I began to fill in the government organizational chart, I noticed many areas were not filled in, like District Council or local Mayors. Afghanistan was scheduled to have District Council elections but they were cancelled until who knows when. So, literally, in Maiwand, there were no Afghan government representatives aside from the District Governor, a Provincial Council Member, and his few workers. I am not talking about the Ministry of Interior like the Afghan National Police or Afghan National Army. This is separate because it deals with security and my main effort was not related to security. When I read about Afghanistan I realized how much control the central government has. It is a unitary country but it was completely centralized and managed from the top. For instance, a Provincial Governor, and District Governor are all appointed. The only representative body that is elected is the Provincial Council. However, Afghan law is written in a way that this Provincial Council has no real influence on decision-making. It is sad, quite frankly. Working at the district level, I noticed how powerless a District Governor could be. He is not elected and only appointed. Therefore, if he wants to stay in power, he is bound and subject to the central government and not so much to the people. So where is the real democracy? The real Afghanistan is a semi-authoritative government, not representative.

But I had to work with what we had and make the best out of

it. So DG Karimi, Team D, Hola, and I met and decided that it is important to at least have a DDA because it would contribute to change people's view on the Afghan government. People in Maiwand didn't trust the Afghan government and this was the Taliban's big push to bring people to the Shadow Government. Although the DDA was not probably representative, the 20 members that were going to be elected represented the major tribes. The role for the 20 members was to bring their tribe's concerns to DG Karimi. I knew that the DDA would also be included in my mentorship, especially of the DDA Chairman. DG Karimi moved forward and the elders elected 20 members that included a Chairman, Deputy Chairman, Clerk, and Treasurer. DG Karimi thanked the DST for supporting the establishment of the DDA. The elders knew that establishing a DDA was important for the development efforts in Maiwand and it would serve as the bridge with the assistance from the military, Afghan government, and DST.

Having a DDA was a big victory for all the key partners in Maiwand because it finally demonstrated that we worked together and made something fruitful happen. It was symbolic, taking into consideration all the problems that existed inside the COP and the District Government. I was very happy because it provided a positive signal for good things that would come to Maiwand. It is probably difficult to understand the level of impact. Sometimes that impact is not measured by the number of projects. I think showing people the right path and seeing that they are taking the initiative adds more to the effect because that output is something that may never disappear. So the fact that Maiwands now had a DDA was symbolic in itself.

Most of the members received a stipend and the moment they were elected they received training from the Ministry Rural Reconstruction and Development (MRRD). Throughout my stories I would continue to mention the MRRD because it was a key institutional player. From a strategic point, I knew that if we could get a DDA in place then Maiwand may have gained access to the National Area Base Development Program (NABDP) Phase III funds program that was ran by CIDA (the Canadian International Development Agency). Later on, we did a big push and were able to grab the last remaining funding available from CIDA to Maiwand. It was a symbolic effort. The MRRD provided me with the Five Year District Development Plan that the DDA compiled with the approval from DG Karimi.

    a. Security Sector – Building of checkpoints.
    b. Governance Rule of Law and Human Rights – DDA members did unidentified projects.
    c. Infrastructure and Natural Resources – Construction of roads that could provide access to natural water and communication.
    d. Education, Media, Sports, and Culture – Building of primary schools and vocational training centers.
    e. Health and Nutrition – Construction of a new clinic and provide 50 hospital beds to the community health clinic.
    f. Agricultural and Rural Development Sector – Provide fertilizers and tractor equipment to farmers. Build an animal clinic in the Hutal center.
    g. Social Protection – Develop technical courses.
    h. Natural Disaster Management – Construction of retaining walls.

It was symbolic to finally have development documents for the district because they would serve as a foundation and be a working tool for everyone. For my team, it was important to begin to do projects that would fall under the Five Year District Development Plan because it would demonstrate that we respected the people's request and that we were not dictating what was best for an Afghan. It was more on our Afghan counterparts to tell us what was best for their district. It was important to me that Afghans became agents of their own development efforts.

Among all the other things on our agenda was to be ready for VIP visits. When there was an Afghan VIP visit we had to be ready to mentor DG Karimi and other Afghan local authorities. The first VIP visit that we had was when a well-known Afghan Parliament member Hero Jabbar visited Maiwand. The purpose of his visit was to inaugurate the Afghan Local Police (ALP). The ALP was a community police force designed to add security support to the Afghan National Police (ANP). The U.S. Army Special Forces worked side by side with the Afghan Special Forces to provide the training. Hero Jabbar brought a high representative from the Ministry of Interior to inaugurate the ALP program. At the ceremony we had the presence of DG Karimi, ISAF, DST, and ANSF. Because this was related to security, I was only an observer and took some notes and pictures. Prior to the ceremony, DG Karimi organized a small Shura with the elders to meet with Hero Jabbar. Hero Jabbar was known in this area for his fighting against the Russians during the Cold War. He was a former Mujahideen and spoke about how he defeated the Russians, and he told the elders that they could defeat the Taliban, too. However, the elders cared more about getting essential services than defeating the Taliban. I guess times had changed. People asked him for things like water and electricity. It was important for him to bring some hope to the elders and assure them that Maiwand could get some assistance. He was in Kabul and probably could bring Maiwand's voice to the Afghan higher ups. But throughout my year, I would realize that many of the Afghan officials who came to Maiwand would talk, talk, and talk. It wasn't their fault; they were probably just frustrated with the system. The Afghan government decentralized system (if it exists) doesn't function well. People didn't expect much from the official visitors. After the small Shura, the ceremony took place and the representative from the Ministry of Interior introduced to the elders how the ALP uniform would look and what the ALP would do for their community. Elders were told that ALP officers would receive trucks, weapons, salaries, and training. This program was a great step toward stabilizing the district.

Then there was the upcoming visit by the Kandahar PG. Since he was the PG, there were high expectations on what he could deliver. As I already explained, we tried to mentor and prepare DG Karimi to have a good engagement with the PG. The PG was going to bring the Directors of Education, Health, and Agriculture. DG Karimi requested he also bring Maiwand's Provincial Council Member. Yes, Maiwand had an elected Provincial Council member but he never really came to Maiwand. The PG traveled by air with ISAF's military helicopters. He also brought with him local media. DG Karimi had a lot of elders present at the Special Shura or Governance, Reconstruction, and Development meeting. I wasn't impressed with the PG. Just like other Afghan officials; he talked a lot and requested that the elders tell his Directors their water, health, and agriculture problems. The Directors would take the elder's requests and those requests would just fall somewhere on top of more requests. Later in the book you will find out how we convinced an Afghan Ministry to provide support to Maiwand, but it felt like pulling teeth. However, for this meeting, there was just a lot of talk by the PG and nothing really significant was added. So for us, it was time to move on and see what we could do as a community. I will not add much more to this section because I get really upset when I saw all the effort the community put into expressing its voice and didn't see deliverables in response.

Launching the first project was going to be tough but my Iraq experience paid off, as I knew how to make work with my military counterparts. As I already mentioned, we had a PSYOPS team with a Radio in a Box (RIAB) in the COP. The radio station in the COP had the capability to reach a good number of villages. So I began to brainstorm about how I could be involved with the radio station. I knew it was important to educate the local population on how the Afghan government works and what was the citizen's role and responsibilities. Later throughout the year, I would expand the radio station with health and rule of law messages. The end goal for the radio messages was good governance civic education. In order for the Maiwand people to understand and appreciate their opportunities and responsibilities as democratic citizens, they needed to receive a sound education. The radio education spots sought not only to familiarize people with the precepts and practices of democracy, but also to produce citizens who are principled, independent, inquisitive, and analytic in their outlook and committed to democracy. It was important for Maiwand citizens to be informed about services they had a right to expect from their district and provincial government and about steps they could take to make themselves heard (such as community councils and petitions). I didn't have experience working with a radio station or how to write radio scripts. It was important for me to be creative about this. I created a radio format where in the beginning I would write an education spot on how the Afghan government functions. For instance, in a section I would describe what is the role of the District Governor or how the District Development Assembly functions. The second section provided a summary of the Shura for the week. The third section provided information on the following week's Shura and ended with a message: "It's your Right, It's your Voice, come to the Shura." I called the governance weekly radio message program *Local Democracy Voices*." I was happy because it was the first governance project and, although it probably sounded small, it provided the proper incentive to continue to move forward. Before we implemented the project, we ran it through DG Karimi to get his okay. I knew it was important to empower DG Karimi and make sure he was aware of what was going on in the District. DG Karimi also came to the radio station several times and sent peaceful messages. This was the first civilian-military project and it was symbolic, considering what happened with Robert and all the chaos.

As we continued to move forward, Team D and Hola began to understand some of the reasons why the district government was so dysfunctional. DG Karimi told Team D, Hola, and I that it was important for him to fill his Tashkiel (civil servant government staff) in order to improve the functionality of the district. The district had nine official representatives from the ministries of education, health, agriculture, electricity, telecom, and civil registry. Half of them actually came to work. Although the problem could've been low salary, I think the main problem is that the Afghan government has failed to resource and task their government employees. For Maiwand, it wasn't so much that the Tashkiel workers didn't want to work, but that the workers didn't know what to do. Only the education, health, and civil registry workers were active in their positions because people came to the clinic, the clinic received some assistance from USAID; the education officers were busy running the Hutal school; and the civil registry worker was always at the District Center because locals approached to him to work on their Tashkeras (identification cards). However, there was another reality that there were workers who, despite the fact that there were programs through which they could assist the people, refused to come to work unless you paid them more money. Even though it was their responsibility as ministry representatives to support all efforts related to their respective ministries. I will give you an example from the agriculture officer and how dysfunctional the Ministry of Agriculture was. A few years ago, the Canadians built a beautiful Agriculture Center in Maiwand. Actually, I heard they built the entire compound, which included the Police Center, District Governor's building, Model Farm, and Agriculture Center. The Agriculture Center was located behind the Model Farm and it had six buildings. Once the construction was completed, the six Agriculture Center buildings were officially transferred to the Ministry of Agriculture. Each building had the same dimensions with a full kitchen and bathroom. Three buildings were fully equipped with air conditioners and furniture. Once the transfer took place, the Ministry of Agriculture promised to fully staff the Agriculture Tashkiel with agriculture officers and provide agriculture programs and the Model Farm and Agriculture Center buildings were going to be play a strong role in agriculture development in Maiwand. Maiwand looked like it was going to become a model of success to other districts. This all sounded great back then but, when I arrived, I found empty buildings and a Model Farm collecting trash. Yes, it was an unfortunate reality. When I first visited the Agriculture Center, I was amazed at how these buildings were unused. Maiwand had two agriculture officers. I heard one showed up once and never came back to the district. The other agriculture representative would only work if you paid him triple his salary. The agriculture representative shouldn't have been paid extra for just doing his job. I was displeased with the lack of funding aid stream from the Afghan government to the province, and from the province to the district. If the Afghan government channeled the appropriate funding stream to the district, Tashkiel workers would be fully occupied in doing work and supporting the people's needs. This was an ideal scenario and it was difficult to see how it would happen in Maiwand. At the rate that the Afghan government was moving forward, I was not sure if they would be ready any time soon to support their district governments. The system was too centralized and the Afghan-subnational officials were not empowered. Getting funds from the Afghan government was very difficult.

It was important for me to learn the funding cycle in Afghanistan. A government cannot function without a budget and certainly the ineffectiveness of the Tashkiel was an example of this. Without the proper development funding budget from the ministries, the Tashkiel workers couldn't function and exercise their positions at the Tashkiel. Maiwand district didn't get development funding in order for them to implement projects. The system is so centralized that when the Afghan government approves its national budget, it is channeled from the Ministry of Finance to the appropriate ministry, which channels the funding to the provinces and then from the provinces to the district. The national budget national programs have sub-programs that could be implemented in the district but unfortunately none of these programs came to Maiwand. We also have to take into consideration that majority of the development funding source is provided by Japan, the World Bank, the U.S., Denmark, France, the Netherlands, etc. I am probably missing a few but the point that I am trying to make is that the funding source must reach all the districts proportionally.

From the personal side, after being in Maiwand for a month, I started to feel more comfortable with the people I was working with. We all began to develop a personal and professional clique. The relations with the military most certainly improved and I felt that I was developing a good informal relationship with DG Karimi. My daily routine began early in the morning. My girlfriend was one of the reasons I made it through my tour in Afghanistan. It was a long tour but she definitely helped me out, although we broke up a month before I completed my tour in Afghanistan and now we are back together. I woke up around 5:00 am and watched a nice Peruvian soap opera; it made me laugh. Then after an hour, I got ready for the day. I always swept my trailer in the morning. By doing this every morning, I felt I was throwing away all the negative things that happened the day before or that I expected to come. I am a bit superstitious. Then I would go to the bathroom and it was very cold. As I already mentioned before, we didn't have real bathrooms. We had latrines and a shower tent. Going to the latrines early in the morning around 6:00 am with freezing rain was a big adjustment. The mornings would be foggy, cloudy, and rainy. In the months of February and March it rains a lot in Maiwand. It rained so much that sometimes water would go through the roof of my trailer. I am glad I brought the sleeping bag that the Embassy provided it me. It was cold but not as cold as Kabul or other places in the north. After I took care of my essentials, I grabbed coffee from the cafeteria tent. Then I would come back to my trailer and get on Skype with my girlfriend and we would talk for about an hour. It was nice to talk to somebody that you love and she knew the moral support was important. After I spoke to her, I went on with my regular daily tasks. On a large board I would write my daily tasks for the week. Usually, Monday and Wednesday would be busy with Shuras at the District Center. On the other days, I would have meetings and conference calls with my military counterparts from other bases. Later in the afternoon, I would give myself at least an hour to do pull ups and walk on the elliptical machine. We had a small gym with the basic exercise machines. After the gym, I always went directly to the shower tent because if I waited later to take a shower, there would not be hot water. I took some cold showers during the winter because we just ran out of hot water. It was all right, I just had to get used to it. I always had to take a shower. Although later in the spring the shower tent sometimes was not working and I just showered with a hose behind my trailer. After I took a shower, I came to the trailer, changed, ate dinner, and then went straight to bed. There were nights when I would stay up for a long time just working, designing best approaches to work for the district. I never stopped doing my lessons learned and finding out what could actually work in Maiwand. I knew that staying focused was essential, especially when you are exposed to violence on a daily basis. Oh yes, I forgot to mention, by now I was officially appointed the Team Leader for all governance and development and was the DST Civilian Lead. I earned the respect of my military counterparts and they were pleased with my commitment in Maiwand. I had to provide myself time to go back and rethink my process:

- I visualized and worked on setting up my goals and how to go about progress. Again, I knew staying focused was important in order to overcome the challenges and work with my counterparts.
- I continued to update my plans on what I needed to do to achieve my goals. I wanted to keep things simple, which would allow me to concentrate on tasks. I recognized that effective time management would be crucial to accomplishing the organizational tasks as well as to avoid wasting valuable organizational assets. In a complex war

environment like Afghanistan and working on the front lines, I began to realize that numerous demands in a limited time would arise.

- I updated my commitments to achieve my goals.
- I continued to set up timeframes in the short-term, medium-term, and long-term. Setting up timeframes allowed me to stay focused on progress. As I got to know the district, I updated my SWOT (Strength, Weaknesses, Opportunities, and Threats) analysis and understood that other factors may come into play.
- I began to adjust priorities as a result of new tasks as requested by the District Government.
- I never stopped setting aside time to reflect on lessons learned.

As you can see, it started to become a bit busy for me. I also tried not to put too much pressure on myself. I knew that moving programs in Afghanistan would become tedious and it would require a lot of patience. But one aspect that I haven't mentioned yet is the security challenges in Maiwand. We lived in a small bubble. Our base in Hutal provided security for its surroundings like the local bazaar. When I was in Iraq, we were used to indirect fire (such as rockets) landing inside the base. For us we didn't have that problem in our COP. We didn't have large speakers that would announce an incoming attack; however, we were still vulnerable to one because of our close proximity to the local population. A mosque was located right outside the COP and some people thought that's why we didn't get attacked. But that wasn't true, as two locals who worked in our COP got shot right outside the COP and in front of the Mosque. I got used to hearing bombs and gunshots; living in Peru in the 1980s, I witnessed the rise of the Shining Path – a well known Maoist terrorist group. They were known for car bombs and drive by shootings. As with Afghanistan, insurgents placed improvised explosive devices (IEDs) along the roads and drive-by shootings were also common. If an IED went off, you could hear it and feel it at the base because it would shake the ground. Many times, our military counterparts would spot an IED and it would be detonated. When an IED got detonated, it would also shake the base. We had a tendency to believe that if a bomb would go off or if there was an attack, it was done by the Taliban. The Taliban got the blame for many of the attacks in Maiwand. However, we also had criminal groups that would attack the coalition. There were too many drugs in Afghanistan and one of the consequences was that people would fight among each other. Tribal relations existed and it was expected to see tribal disputes. I think Afghanistan is a combination of everything, which at the end destabilizes the country. Psychologically, you have to prepare yourself for this tough assignment. When you are in rural Afghanistan you are at risk and have to accept that there is violence and if you are at the wrong place at the wrong time you might never come home. I accepted this reality when I took on this assignment. I knew that every time I went outside the base to go to the District Center, even with all the body armor that I had, if a sniper wanted to kill me they could've done it easily. Whenever I walked outside the base, I wore my helmet, protective vest, and had a secure GPS tracker. I always had security when I walked outside the base. I have to thank my military counterparts for providing security. But again, if it was your day and time to go, then so be it. I know it sounds very harsh but this was a reality.

Towards the end of February I was asked to attend a conference in Area A. Over in Area A we were going to have other DSTs, military counterparts, and other key players of the U.S. Mission in Southern Afghanistan. I wasn't sure if I wanted to attend because I knew how difficult it was going to be to get there from Maiwand. Flights didn't get supported much to Maiwand so once you left Maiwand, boy, you had to pack for a couple of days because many things could happen and you could be stuck in Area A for days. I was asked to bring my military colleagues and I brought Team D team leader Hawaii and Hola. Actually, the fact that they went to the conference with me demonstrated our good relations with our military counterparts. When I arrived, I still didn't know many of the folks in Area A. I felt relatively new and was more of an observer. The conference lasted for two days and I didn't find any substance in it.

It is funny, the ghost of Robert continued to haunt me through February. I have another anecdote. The last day of the conference, the KT asked all the DSTs to introduce their team and as people went around the coordinator for the conference forgot to call on Maiwand. So I raised my hand and said "Hey don't forget about Maiwand because we are here present." I was a bit upset because so many negative things had been said about Maiwand, that there was no hope that the district could turnaround. I thought that it was important to send a positive message. So I got up and I introduced my military colleagues. Everyone looked at me weird like, who is this guy? And what is Maiwand? It seemed like Maiwand was off the radar despite the fact that the military had big plans for Maiwand in 2011. Later on you will find out what happened to those promises. I was excited that there were big plans for Maiwand but, based on my Iraq experience, I took those promises very cautiously. For instance, when I was in Iraq, in the southern province, my military counterparts had many plans to reignite the local economy with large-scale projects. However, the military functions like any other federal bureaucracy and problems with the funding can happen. Many promises were made but, due to funding issues, many of the promises never turned out to be projects. This is the reason why I keep saying to start small and don't jump to promises and build expectations that can't be fulfilled. I told everyone that I was the DST State Department Representative and told them briefly my funny anecdote about when Robert came to my training and I told myself that I hope I didn't go to Maiwand. I told everyone that people should not be scared of visiting us and that we are re-establishing a foundation where we could be on track with the governance and development efforts. People looked at me and I saw this guy laughing. I tried to send a positive message. After my speech, my military counterparts supported my positive message by telling everyone that we were working on the relations and things were looking better. When my military counterparts threw their support to me, I knew I was on the right track. As you know, I wanted to begin to rebuild the working relations with my military counterparts. I knew that the relationship between the DST and my Afghan counterparts was improving. After the speech by my military counterparts, I approached the KT Director and provided him with an update on how things were in Maiwand. He didn't seem to really care and was more interested in finding out when our DG was leaving. I told him that I could probably turn DG Karimi around and we could mentor him. All those reports that were written about DG Karimi were probably exaggerated. I was still told that the PG was going to remove DG Karimi. I tried to convince him that there was something positive that we could do and turnaround DG Karimi. Still, for the people at the KT, Maiwand was falling apart and there was nothing left to do. I told the KT director that I would still move forward with what we have and if there is a new District Governor, then so be it and we would work with it. I advised the KT Director that if there was going to be a replacement we shouldn't do it when there was major transition of key players. Later on you will see that we had a District Governor replacement but this didn't take place until the end of my tour. Good mentorship was important for our Afghans; unfortunately, through my year, I realized that there wasn't good mentorship in Kandahar City. In Kandahar City, we had the provincial authorities. I left the conference somewhat upset because I felt I had no support from the KT and they didn't seem to really care for the work that we were doing. But I still moved forward, with or without their support. My ultimate goal was to assist Maiwand and turnaround the district. I was put on this assignment and I wasn't going to let down my Afghan counterparts and team members. I didn't come to Afghanistan to collect paychecks. I came to Afghanistan to make a difference and win the people's hearts and mind. My goal was to show the local populace that America really cares about Afghanistan.

The first project (*Local Democracy Voices*) by the DST paved the way to begin thinking critically and deciding how to go about bringing some local NGOs to work in Maiwand. As I mentioned before, it was important for the DST to show that it would do the mentoring. Mentorship was an important aspect but you also want to make sure you complete a project because it would not only empower my Afghan counterparts but it would also empower *me*. By doing a project you also find out how your Afghan counterparts would behave knowing that there is funding coming to the district. In this type of environment, the locals didn't care as much about mentorship as they do about projects. You must balance your work and expectations for your district. For my team that I had begun to lead, it was important to do both – mentorship and projects. Proper balance brings better outputs. I couldn't believe how time was going by so quickly, and it was important that I had something going on before the beginning of Spring 2011. One of the assets we had was the U.S. Embassy funds, which could be used to fund community projects. We didn't have local NGOs in Maiwand. In contrast with my experience in Iraq, where I had money available to do direct implementation for a project, in Afghanistan I needed an implementing partner to do the project on my behalf. Boy, when I found out about this rule I really scratched my head. I knew it would be difficult to make something happen with the U.S. Embassy funds, knowing that there were no local NGOs. It was possible to mentor some people on how an NGO works but there were too many procedures to have the NGO registered with the Ministry of Economy. There was a high illiteracy rate in Maiwand and the elders were very old. I knew that in order to do a project I needed active, young Afghans. It was hard to find them because we were sucked into working in a bubble around our COP. Scramble and I couldn't travel outside this bubble because of the security situation. There were big expectations to expand from the bubble we were stuck in, but we didn't. In Kandahar City, the capital of Kandahar Province, you had a large literacy rate and all 29 Afghan local NGOs were located there. Most of them had worked with the Canadians. I sent an email to each of the NGOs and for many days I had no response. I am sure they were skeptical on who I was and whether the email was actually coming from me. So I decided to resend the email and after a couple of days I began to receive responses from the NGOs. The majority of them told me that they couldn't come to Maiwand because of the security situation. There was, among Kandaharis, the perception that Maiwand was not completely secure. Out of the 29 NGOs that we invited, only 5 decided to attend an NGO meeting that we organized in early March.

The NGO meeting was organized during the Development Shura with the elders. It was challenging and very difficult for the elders to understand what an NGO was. Many thought that an NGO was a construction company, and the elders kept mentioning that they have contractors that could build roads and water dams. I had a feeling we were going to have this discussion so before the meeting I printed the rules and guidelines for an NGO in Pashto. I knew this confusion was coming because DG Karimi appeared confused when I had the opportunity to talk to him about the upcoming NGO meeting. When the NGOs came to the district, all the elders, DDA, and DG Karimi were skeptical about their work. Just by looking at how the NGO reps dressed you could tell they had a better education and life than the elders from Maiwand. The elders would get very upset when one of the reps would use the term "NGO" to refer to their organization. The elders would stop and request that the NGO rep speak in Pashto words and not to mix English and Pashto words. It was important that the NGOs came to Maiwand because they were going to play a key role for the DST. In order for the DST to use U.S. Embassy funds, we had to use a local Afghan NGO. I didn't like this rule because it was difficult to provide oversight knowing that we couldn't really get out too much because of the security. However, later you will find out how we did our first project and set it up in a way where we had a lot of eyes on it. Having eyes on the project is important because if something goes wrong, the donor will be the one that needs to respond. The five NGOs that came to Maiwand spoke on their previous activities with several international aid agencies such as USAID and CIDA. The members all spoke English. After each NGO introduced their organization, I stood up in front of the elders and spoke about how the DST, through its U.S. Embassy funds, would work with a local NGO to implement a project. I listed the type of projects that we could do such as vocational training. Almost all the elders requested water and electricity as the primary need. I told them that we couldn't do infrastructure projects because it required a lot of funding. Furthermore, we were moving away from infrastructure projects because it was important for the Afghan government to take the lead on them - It was more sustainable that way. A lot of the elders then told me that they didn't need an NGO because a vocational training was probably a waste of time. The problem in Maiwand was not lack of water but poor water management. People in Maiwand didn't know how to manage the water and lot of water gets wasted. I told this to the elders and they all looked at me as if they agreed. The DDA Chairman was still skeptical of the NGOs as they wanted to have full control of the activities. I told the DDA Chairman that it was important for us to have the DDA involved with the elders as we tried to educate the community on how to do projects. I highlighted the four Community Learning and Development Approaches that we were using to assist them:

   a. Empowerment – Increase the ability of DG Karimi, DDA, and village groups.
   b. Participation – Support the DDA, DG Karimi, and elders to take part in the decision-making.
   c. Self-determination – Support the right of people to make their own choices.

d. Partnership – Recognize the Afghan government, ISAF, DST, and other key partners contribution to community learning and development, and should work together to make the most of the resources available and be as effective as possible.

I still had some challenges convincing everyone that we were here to help with the local NGOs. At one point the DDA, DG Karimi, and elders told me that they didn't want the Kandahar City NGOs to work in Maiwand because they prefer people from Maiwand to be hired. Just like any small community, people were biased and didn't want outsiders. I told the elders, no problem, we could work with a Maiwand local NGO. The problem was that we didn't have a local NGO in Maiwand. They told me that they have only construction companies. Again I scratched my head and reminded them that we didn't fund construction companies. I told the Shura members that the only way a DST could directly fund a project for Maiwand was through the NGOs. Again, I showed them an official Ministry of Economy certificate in Pashto that listed the NGO registration. Finally, DG Karimi told the DDA and elders the importance of working with the local NGO because it could be of assistance for the community. The NGO was instructed to vet the project with the elders, DG, and DDA. After vetting the project, the NGO would come to the DST and discuss what the community wants. The elders and DDA still questioned how the NGOs worked. I stood up again and told everyone that if they didn't want the NGOs in Maiwand, then it was fine with me and that it was most likely they would not see a direct project from the DST. Suddenly, the elders, DDA, and DG Karimi agreed to have the NGOs and from there we went forward with the engagement. Just like the Afghans, I could play hardball. I think it is the reason why I earned the respect from my Afghan counterparts. I played a fair game with them.

As we continued to move forward with the NGOs, we also continued to move forward with the mentorship. Team D, Hola, and I met again DG Karimi to discuss his budget request. In Afghanistan their fiscal year starts in March and ends the following year in February. Afghanistan goes by the solar year so it was a critical point, to find out how much money Maiwand would receive in March under the 1390 fiscal budget (March 2011 – February 2012 is known as 1390.) By early March there was nothing in the budget and Team D, Hola, and the DST wanted to find out more about the process, like how money is requested from the district and channeled to the provincial level. We were very impressed on how knowledgeable DG Karimi was on the budget process. His budget request was the same as the Five Year District Development Plan priorities he explained to us before. For this year 1390 District Budget, DG Karimi requested construction of new schools and clinics, transfer of the Kajaki power to the Maiwand district, provision of alternative crops to farmers, and monthly meetings with the Director of Health and Education in Maiwand. DG Karimi was very skeptical that the Afghan government would help Maiwand. I was also very skeptical about how much money would flow through the district, especially taking into consideration how dysfunctional the Afghan government was. DG Karimi was aware that the Provincial Line Ministry Directors in Kandahar City had a tendency to amend his budget request. Below were some of the common complaints during the submission of the budget:

a. Poor communication and coordination
   - External projects were not coordinated with central and provincial government.
   - Ministries budget didn't reflect the district priorities.
b. Poor Execution
   - Kandahar officials lacked the capacity to understand the planning and budgetary process.
c. Unfair Allocation
   - Line Ministry Directors used an ad hoc or historical approach to allocate budget.

As you can see from the above example, as we tried to build good governance in Maiwand, we were confronted with a large scope of problems from the Kabul and Kandahar level. Our work would not be enough if the Afghan "Centralized" government didn't do much to assist and empower its local officials. There was nothing more a District Governor could do beyond sending his request. The system was so centralized that a District Governor couldn't do much to raise his voice. At the provincial level, even the provincial authorities probably would not be heard by their Kabul Afghan counterparts. We were at the lowest of the low according to the Afghan government hierarchy and seeing how policy is pushed down or literally stuck somewhere in Kabul was very disappointing. I was able to get a hold of the 1390 national budget and I was upset to see how much money was provided to Afghanistan but it never reached Maiwand. It was important not only for the district government officials to be active in their roles but also for the provincial and Kabul officials. Afghanistan is a top down system, not a bottom up system. There was nothing much we could do from the ground without assistance from the provincial-level authorities. Kabul was too far for us but it was the role of the provincial authorities to communicate the message to Kabul, and they continued to fail.

As part of the strategy to continue to promote economic and political development, I began to draw from my development experience. I recognized that a program to support economic and political development in a dynamic and unpredictable environment is a complex process that carries risks. I knew that a well-developed and understood strategic vision and policy could help to get the most from our efforts and reduce the risks by providing a framework and guidance for our initiatives. To maximize our resources we decided to target these core competency areas, which would assist in building a self-sustaining, representative, and accountable local government:

1. Operating Tashkiel

    a. Contact the current civil servants and resolve the issue of their absence.
    b. Mentor DG Karimi to enforce the civil servants to report at least twice a week.
    c. Request the civil servants to attend the Development Shura.
    d. Request the respective Line Ministry Director in Kandahar City and Independent Directorate of Local Governance (IDLG) to make a replacement if civil servants didn't show to work.
    e. Facilitate a meeting with the IDL representative to discuss filling the Tashkiel.

2. Government Effectiveness

    a. Mentor DG Karimi on policy reform, institutional development, and implementation.
    b. Mentor the DDA on how to prioritize develop, implement, and monitor projects.
    c. Inform on a weekly basis DG Karimi and DDA on policy issues that may impact Maiwand.
    d. Educate DG Karimi on transparency and accountability. The DST would organize a district governance road tour to small villages and have DG Karimi engage.

3. Decentralized / Support with Line Ministry Representatives

    a. Mentor DG Karimi to contact the Line Ministry Directors and invite them to Maiwand to develop a plan on how to address the people needs.
    b. Advise DG Karimi on how to prioritize which Line of Ministry representatives are in most need in Maiwand.

4. Civil Society Development

   a. Bring local Kandahar City NGOs to Maiwand to engage with local villages in economic and political development projects. It was important for local villagers to identify development needs. We considered collaboration with the local NGOs important because of their responsiveness, innovation, direct relationship with the poor, capacity to stimulate participation and articulate local views, cost effectiveness, local accountability and independent assessment of issues.
   b. Request U.S Embassy funds.
   c. Task NGOs with empowering the local community and enforcing participation.
   d. Engage the NGOs with DG Karimi and DDA.

5. Develop Civic Responsibility

   a. Radio in a Box -Maiwand *"Local Democracy Voices"* – A governance civic education outreach to the local villages in order for people to understand and appreciate their opportunities and responsibilities as democratic citizens. Educating citizens about democracy should not be viewed as an isolated subject, taught for a short time each day and otherwise ignored. In order for the Maiwand people to understand and appreciate their opportunities and responsibilities as democratic citizens, they needed to receive a sound education. Good democracy education in Maiwand would be part of good education in general.
   b. Transfer the development Shura at least once a month to a village location whereby villagers could be acquainted with the projects that the Afghan government, military, and DST are implementing. DG Karimi would educate the

local villagers on their responsibilities and rights as a citizen to participate in a local Shura.

I couldn't come up with these competency areas when I first arrived in Maiwand. It took me a couple of weeks and lot of dedication to push myself to understand the local environment. Doing my homework and research paid off because these priorities were well received by my counterparts from Area A and the KT. All these priorities were never really changed throughout my entire tour in Afghanistan. This demonstrated that I provided a good assessment and had a good vision for the district. Most important, I knew that I was providing good mentorship to DG Karimi. But, being the nerd that I am, I didn't stop and continued to develop tools that would help assist the district with the governance conditions. I developed a subjective governance radar chart to track the governance status of the district. I followed the World Bank six governance dimensions to develop the governance radar chart. The information that I used to update that governance radar chart was based on opinions, observations, projects, and engagements. The DST in Maiwand was the first one to do something like this. I did it primarily because there was no way to understand the local government conditions. Throughout the year on a quarterly basis, I would update the governance radar chart.

1. *Voice and Accountability* – Assess how the Maiwand citizens are able to participate in selecting their local government.
2. *Political Stability* – Assess what is the chance that the local government would be destabilized by the Insurgency.
3. *Government Effectiveness* – Assess perceptions of quality of public services and administration.
4. *Regulatory Quality* – Assess the ability on how the District Government could formulate and implement sound policies that permit economic development.
5. *Rule of Law* – Assess how Maiwand abided by the rules of society, police, and the courts.

6. *Control of Corruption* – Assess corruption activities by powerbrokers.

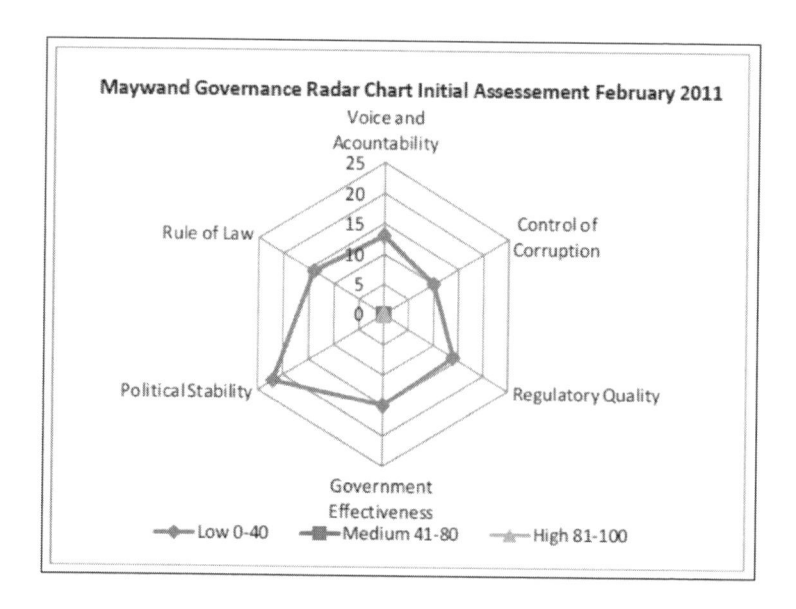

Maywand Governance Radar Chart Initial Assessement February 2011

(Radar chart with axes: Voice and Acountability, Control of Corruption, Regulatory Quality, Government Effectiveness, Political Stability, Rule of Law; scale 0–25; legend: Low 0-40, Medium 41-80, High 81-100)

My first assessment wasn't very positive for the district. I knew there were many things to be done for the district.

Voice and Accountability – Community members didn't come to the District Center very often and there was a sense of distrust on the Afghan government officials.

Political Stability – Because the District Government building was located next to our base it was difficult for the insurgents to assault the government officials although the risk was always high.

Government Effectiveness – DG Karimi wasn't moving projects per se with the Afghan government. There was no linkage with the provincial government officials.

Regulatory Quality – DG Karimi didn't have in place a sound policy where he can regulate the effectiveness of the district government.

DG Karimi was aware of the national and provincial policies but these policies never really made it to the district in order for him to provide the proper regulatory quality. Policies in economic development never made it to Maiwand. If it did, it only made it with the assistance of international organizations.

Rule of Law – We didn't have a judge and attorney general. To solve this issue, DG Karimi acted as the mediator to solve the community disputes. We only had a National Director Security (NDS) prosecutor officer who focus primarily on insurgent cases.

Control of Corruption – It is very difficult to assess the level of corruption in Maiwand. However, we assumed the level of corruption was extremely high in Maiwand. For this reason, I couldn't really judge the appropriate level.

By the end of my tour, we had some gains but there was still much to be done. Unfortunately, one of the continuous struggles that I had to go through was the "government effectiveness," because building governance in Maiwand was so challenging. For me, creating tools was very important. You could see that working with priorities and a radar chart was not enough for me. I also developed this framework (see below) to assist me on how to handle the governance efforts. It was quite difficult to achieve the outputs and outcomes but I think when I left Maiwand it was in a better position to function. You can't change a system in one year. I think we were able to mentor satisfactorily our counterparts by working from the lower level, with the hope that they could continue by themselves. We were in an infant democracy and local and provincial policymakers would continue to make mistakes. The tools that I developed were important because if something bad happens or we detour an objective, a proper tool could guide us back to the proper direction.

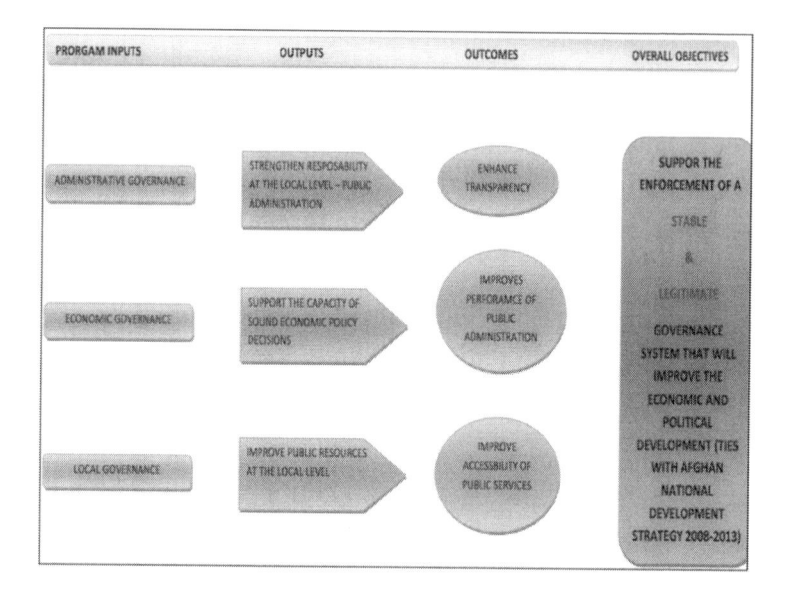

PROGRAM INPUTS	OUTPUTS	OUTCOMES	OVERALL OBJECTIVES
ADMINISTRATIVE GOVERNANCE	STRENGTHEN RESPONSABILITY AT THE LOCAL LEVEL – PUBLIC ADMINISTRATION	ENHANCE TRANSPARENCY	SUPPORT THE ENFORCEMENT OF A STABLE & LEGITIMATE GOVERNANCE SYSTEM THAT WILL IMPROVE THE ECONOMIC AND POLITICAL DEVELOPMENT (TIES WITH AFGHAN NATIONAL DEVELOPMENT STRATEGY 2008-2013)
ECONOMIC GOVERNANCE	SUPPORT THE CAPACITY OF SOUND ECONOMIC POLICY DECISIONS	IMPROVES PERFORMANCE OF PUBLIC ADMINISTRATION	
LOCAL GOVERNANCE	IMPROVE PUBLIC RESOURCES AT THE LOCAL LEVEL	IMPROVE ACCESSIBILITY OF PUBLIC SERVICES	

By March I had made a lot of progress in terms of learning the programs, the government, and the local politics. Another example of my educational experience was to research how the education program functioned in Maiwand. The educational system in rural Afghanistan is not good. Human capital is extremely low and I would find myself with adults and children who were illiterate. One day, Hola, Scramble, and I went to the school located next to our base and met with the Director of Education for Maiwand. The purpose of the meeting was to find out the status of the schools and the problems they were having. He told us that three schools had reopened. Two schools were located in a guesthouse because the Ministry of Education didn't want the Taliban to find it. The fourth school was the formal one and it was located next to our base. We called it the Hutal School. Nothing happened to that school because the insurgents knew that we would respond to any attacks. Rumor was that in the Hutal School, the Taliban had one of its first meetings to officially organize their insurgent organization and planned attacks throughout Kandahar Province from there. The DST asked if the schools were receiving support from Afghan Government. Both education officers told me that they were receiving some support but it wasn't enough. The Taliban threat in the villages continued and teachers didn't want to teach the children. One of the education officers who oversaw the payment to the teachers and provided school supplies told me that once the Taliban intercepted him on his way to one of the guesthouses. According to him, the Taliban asked him for the teachers' salaries and questioned him on why he was working for the Afghan government. The Taliban told him that he was a traitor and he was taken to a small prison cell in a house and beaten for days. He was taken out of Kandahar Province and found himself in the north. He was able to escape and finally returned to Maiwand. However, he said that unless we did something to control the insurgent activity, the education efforts would remain stalled in Maiwand. But it was also important to know that, for many Afghans in Maiwand, education for their children is not a top priority. I began to notice when I asked people about their problems, the two main things they would say is water and electricity. When I asked the elders about education, they said "Oh, yes, education, we need more schools." Some Afghans liked the idea of building schools because they could get their hands on contracts that way. But in reality, I didn't think there was any intent to send their children to school. I never saw the school near our base crowded with children. The children would play, ask you for food, pump water from the well, or carry groceries for their families. I saw all of this during the school year. There was no desire to send the children to school, even at the Hutal school, despite the fact that it was secure enough. The Director of Education for Maiwand claimed to have 900 students, but my own estimate was a maximum of 70 students and definitely no more than 100. The Hutal School had many empty classrooms and about 13 students per classroom of the ones that were occupied. When I visited the Hutal School, many of the children were carrying United

Nations Children's Fund school bags, so I knew they received some type of assistance. USAID also assisted with the refurbishment of the school, but for Afghans sometimes it was not enough. They would continue to ask you for more, even if you told them that you didn't have any more funds to support another project.

The security situation in Maiwand was not great. I've mentioned before that we were secure in our surroundings but if you went outside our secure bubble, the situation would worsen. With all the force that we had, the Taliban and other insurgents continued to have control of several areas like Band I Timor, which was located in Maiwand. The insurgents continue to put improvised explosive devices (IEDs) on the roads and in the neighborhood right next to us. We had a large camera where we monitored activities around our COP, but still insurgents had the capacity to place IEDs. When an IED went off, the sound was very loud and the wave would shake my trailer. Your heart starts beating quickly because of the impact. I remember one night around 1:00 am, insurgents threw a couple of grenades to the COP. The grenades landed at the other side of the COP and luckily nobody got hurt. I was close by when the grenade attack occurred but I didn't get hurt. I was getting a drink at the cafeteria tent and as soon as I left, the grenades went off. But this was the type of life that I lived in the base. Sometimes we would find IEDs and detonate them. The detonation sound is very loud and would also shake my trailer. I got used to the sounds and knew the difference between a detonation and when an IED went off. In Iraq, when I lived in an FOB, the insurgents would shoot rockets at the base and I didn't know where the rocket would hit. The rocket could've landed anywhere at the base and if it wasn't your day, you would be gone. One afternoon, I was having lunch with Scramble, and suddenly we heard a large explosion and saw the smoke in the air. The Taliban placed an IED at an ANP checkpoint. The explosion killed a few children and a boy lost his leg. Whenever somebody was badly injured, the ANP would take the victim to our base because the community health clinic didn't have the proper equipment to treat someone with severe wounds. If the victim was badly injured, our medics' tent would call up for a helicopter and the victim would be medically evacuated. Throughout the month of March, I saw many medical helicopters coming to our COP to pick up body bags or people who were badly injured. I think psychologically it could impact somebody because these were innocent people. We also risked being shot whenever we left the COP. As I already mentioned, at the COP we had a laundry boy and one cooker get shot at when they left the COP. The military would hire some locals to work at the COP and insurgents would keep track of them. It was a late afternoon, when the cooker and laundry boy left the COP and suddenly two individuals in motorcycles approached them and shot them. They survived the wounds. One was shot in the leg and the other one was shot in the arm. Survival was very difficult in Maiwand; it was much more dangerous than Iraq.

Another large problem in Afghanistan is drug production. In Maiwand, poppy is the engine of the local economy. We had an informal economy with small shopkeepers; however, that was not enough for someone to feed his family. A farmer would get into the poppy production because he could make twice the amount of money in a few months rather than raising legitimate crops. We had an imported local economy and the farmers didn't produce for local market trade. The farmers produced for self-consumption. Everything that was consumed and sold at the local market was imported. Farmers were usually paid in advance in exchange for their work at the poppy fields. The farmers had a specific goal that they needed to meet and when they didn't, the farmer remained in debt until he paid the trader with poppy. Poppy production finances the Taliban. Therefore, it has a lot of interest in districts like Maiwand to continue to produce. Many of the farmers didn't have bad intentions, they only did it to make money. The Afghan government hasn't done anything in Maiwand to assist and provide the farmers with alternative livelihoods. The PG visited again at the end of March to do his Spring poppy eradication activity. There was no coalition presence during the poppy eradication as it was important to show that the Afghan government wanted to do something to fix poppy production. When the PG came to Maiwand he spoke briefly to the elders on how poppy is illegal and how it goes against Islam. The farmers challenged the PG because they were not provided with any assistance and were furious with his preaching. No assistance had been provided to them for years. The farmers were also angry at the PG because the poppy eradication activity would take place in farms that were not of his tribe. The PG was a Norzooi and the poppy eradication activities that took place were in non-Norzooi. The Norzooi tribe is one of the largest tribes in Afghanistan. It was very common that all political appointees such as the District Governor were part of the Norzooi tribe. In Kandahar Province the Norzooi tribe runs the provincial government. We had other tribes in Maiwand, like the Kuchi tribe. It was very common for all tribe members to engage in poppy production. The PG could've done the poppy eradication outside our COP where Norzooi tribe members had large poppy fields but it didn't happen. The poppy eradication did happen; however, in the Kuchi tribes land. This method of tribal bias for eradication upset the Kuchis, as well as members of other tribes. So this poppy eradication activity had its own tribal politics. Even though I didn't spend much time in Maiwand, I understood the farmers' anger because the Afghan government would come and talk to them to eradicate poppy but no assistance was provided. The big question was that if poppy was eradicated from their land, how would the farmer support their families? In Maiwand, a farmer didn't have food to feed the animals so there was no livestock. I mean, we had sheep and goats but farmers would feed them with garbage or whatever was out there. When the farmers asked me for assistance, I would tell them that I didn't have the resources. It was true because the resources to assist a farmer require a large assistance. I am of the opinion that if we have to help out the farmers, this assistance has to come from a large push from the Afghan government. A large countrywide agriculture program was needed. We assisted the farmers with small stuff like training and provided seeds and trees (pomegranate and almond saplings), but we all knew that it wasn't enough.

Towards the end of March and beginning of April, I began to understand and feel more comfortable working in the district. I started to get a good grip on who were the powerbrokers, and the locals would call me by my first name. But another change was coming soon: we were going to get a new military unit, which meant, we would have to start all over again. The new military unit would have their own plans and I knew it was going to be another adjustment. But before this adjustment, I knew I was going to go on my first R&R and I was looking forward to spend time with my girlfriend, friends, and family. I really looked forward to my first leave, but I worked up to the last minute before I left Maiwand. I knew that it was important to leave something for the team to work on.

I have mentioned the idea of empowering the locals with projects. After we brought in the local NGOs, several of them never came back to Maiwand. I think many felt that Maiwand's elders were a bit hostile in terms of the engagement. I didn't blame them because I was at the meeting where the elders were hostile to the NGOs that we invited and many didn't understand their role. There was one NGO that decided to move forward with us in Maiwand. I will call this NGO "WP." WP was an NGO that had experience working with other implementing partners and coalition forces. I will continue to come back and talk about WP and the activity that we did with them. One of the requirements for an NGO to work in Maiwand and receive our funds was to engage with DG Karimi, elders, and DDA. I wanted to push for transparency and accountability, which I noticed was lacking in Maiwand. So WP engaged with the elders, DDA, and DG Karimi.

WP told the DST that they received 50 proposals and narrowed the 50 proposals down to 8 proposals that included:

- Health sanitation training for the Hutal high school
- Health sanitation training for women
- Masonry training
- Build volleyball and basketball court for the Hutal School
- Water drilling
- Tailoring training
- Women livestock training
- Canal cleaning

We arranged a development working group meeting among all key players including DG Karimi and DDA to discuss the above requests. I will continue to come back later on the development working group meeting because it created a strong synchronization of our development efforts. At the first development working group meeting we discussed what was realistic on the type of projects the Embassy would fund and, most importantly, if it was feasible for the district and if these projects were something that Afghans really wanted. I never wanted to impose. It was important to spread the impact as much as possible. The DST reemphasized to the DDA and DG Karimi that the DST couldn't fund large infrastructure projects. The DST informed again the DDA and DG Karimi the projects that we could fund such as education and cultural events/activities, vocational training, civic cleanup activities, purchasing materials gear at capacity training, women's activities, etc. The DST would not fund infrastructure projects that required drafting of plans or oversight by technical engineers (example: roads, buildings, and graveling of roads), duplicated projects that have already been implemented by the military or the Afghan government, and other projects that the Afghan government planned to implement. The scope of work that WP submitted for the trainings had a good background and activities. Rather than funding several technical trainings separately, the DST discussed with DG Karimi and DDA on how to convert one of the new Agriculture Center buildings into a Vocational Training Center (VTC). DG Karimi welcomed the idea and he realized that it was important to begin to utilize the vacant buildings. All the trainings would be conducted at the VTC. The VTC was important because it would strengthen the role of GIRoA by providing a learning environment and enable Maiwands to become better equipped to play a leadership role when they return to their villages. Trainees could share what they had learned, whether it was reading, writing, health and hygiene techniques, or even how to make decisions as a group. Once MRRD funds are transferred to Maiwand, the DDA would link the trainees with the reconstruction projects by providing jobs; and other reconstruction projects that are not Afghan government led whereby donors would have the ability to hire the trainees.

I knew that a VTC would play a role to help Maiwands make the most of the employment opportunities. Without any major industries near the Maiwand District, possibilities for sustainable income generation outside agriculture are minimal. Because of this, unemployment is high among the rural youth who haven't migrated to the major cities in Afghanistan. And because of financial problems, many Maiwands drop out of school before finishing their formal education. This VTC would be set up as a pilot project to give opportunities not only to the youth but to women and everyone in Maiwand to learn a skill and increase their chances to find non-agricultural income generating possibilities. I was very pleased that we were moving forward with this effort because it would not only empower the Afghans but also empower us as a team because, finally, something was about to be done. What made this outreach effort symbolic was the sense of partnership and engagement that linked the Afghan government, community, local leadership, elders, DST, and military. Everyone worked together for a good cause.

Just before I left for R&R, the KT requested another

governance and development meeting. I knew I was more prepared to give a good read out on the district situation than I had been in February. I also had Scramble in Maiwand to support me with the preparation of the presentation. All of my military counterparts were present this time to do the presentation. We did it through videoconference and I think it went well. After the presentation, I was getting ready for my first R&R because I felt that so much had happened since I started the assignment that it was important to sit back and reflect on lessons learned. But I barely made it out of Maiwand. I will never forget this anecdote. I reserved a seat at a military ring route for Thursday. My flight from Dubai was leaving on Monday. At that time the military started to support our base with ring routes. Ring routes means that a helicopter goes around different bases picking up people. A black hawk helicopter could load 11 people depending on how many suitcases people would bring. You're out of luck if the helicopter comes to your base and does not have space any more. The weather was getting pretty bad before Thursday. When the weather goes red (meaning bad visibility) then the helicopters would not fly. I was getting worried thinking that if the weather continues to be bad, the helicopter would not come Thursday and it could really screw my R&R. I could find myself stuck in Maiwand for many days. Also, I was worried because the current unit was about to go through a RIP/TOA and I knew assets would be used for the outgoing unit. A RIP/TOA stands for Relieve in Place and Transfer of Authority. It is when one military unit replaces another in a theatre or area of operations. Of course the flight got cancelled for Thursday. I had three days to think how the hell I was going to get to KAF by Monday. There were no convoys scheduled to KAF. Friday is a bad day to fly because the majority of helicopters didn't fly on a Friday. The other two large bases that were close to me, Azizullah and Ramrod, had no movements until Tuesday of the next week. So I started to unpack thinking that I would not make it to my R&R. I was a bit down Thursday afternoon. I spoke to Hola and he told me to not give up. Early on in the week that I wanted to leave Maiwand, a couple of contractors came to fix one of the cell towers. Contractors could get dedicated military flights. They came directly to Maiwand and it didn't seemed like they were going to stay for a long time. The next day (Friday), I see the four contractors walking to our landing zone like they were waiting for somebody to come and pick them up. It was around 2:42 pm (I still remember the time) when I began to hear a helicopter. I got so used to hearing helicopters that I could tell when one is coming. Sooner or later, I see a military helicopter landing and as is coming down, Hola comes out of his building and tells me "Carlos get your shit together and I will run to the flight line and ask the pilot if they have space for you." Scramble heard it and came out to help me out. I was wearing my pajamas already and didn't have time to change. I put all my stuff in my luggage and my protective vest and ran like I'd never run in my life with so much weight on. When I got to the flight line, I saw Hola talking to the pilot and the pilot gave a thumbs up and I was good to go. It was plain luck that I made it out.

When I got to KAF, I noticed that I was wearing my pajamas and had nothing else to wear. So, no kidding, I wore my pajamas for three days in KAF and then flew to the U.S. in my pajamas. When I got to the U.S. at Washington Dulles Airport the immigration customs officer looked at me and began to ask me questions. He asked me where I was coming from and I told him that I was coming from Afghanistan. He looked at me weird because he noticed I was wearing my pajamas and I looked jetlag and tired. I told him that I barely made it out of my base and I was in such a rush to get out that I didn't have the chance to put on my jeans. He was laughing. Something similar happened when I left again on my second R&R but I will write about it in the next section. It was good to be back home in America and I literally jumped into my bed and fell asleep for hours. The days went by quickly and soon it was time to go back to Afghanistan again. Going back to Afghanistan was always difficult because in a way it seemed so far away and you could be so disconnected with the world that it seemed unreal.

The entrance of my base Combat Operation Outpost Rath.

Weekly meeting with DG Karimi, DDA, and military to discuss development projects.

Putting a smile with the Deputy Director of Education, students, and my military counterpart.

The DDA Chairman leading the DDA Shura.

Traveling to Maiwand.

Always next to DG Karimi as his close adviser, inspecting the progress at the model farm.

Eating Afghan lunch with DG Karimi, ISAF, and ANSF.

Donation of pomegranate trees to the elders at the model farm.

Maiwand

Maiwand local market.

IV

ROAD TO RECOVERY

    Finally, I was on my way back to Afghanistan. I would fly from Washington Dulles to Dubai, then to Kandahar City. When I landed in Dubai, I had to transfer to Terminal 2 for the regional flights. At Terminal 2, the regional flights included Qatar, Iraq, Iran, Afghanistan, Kuwait, etc. I was used to traveling through Terminal 2 whenever I left Iraq. We flew on a contractor airline and the airline made several stops before I reached KAF. We stopped first at Bagram base and then the final stop was KAF. When I arrived at KAF I found out that Osama Bin Laden got killed. There was a lot of joy for those of us who are fighting this war to improve the lives of the Afghans, who have seen so much violence. I was pleased to hear the news also for everyone in America. My girlfriend contacted me and asked me if I was doing okay because the day that I landed in Afghanistan it was the day when Osama Bin Laden got killed. I told her that I was fine. Now I had to resolve how I would get back to Hutal – Maiwand. Flights were not going to Maiwand and we had a new military unit. I spoke with Scramble and he told me that the best bet was to go to FOB Ramrod and from there catch a ground convoy to Hutal. Scramble was going to speak to the new BSO to get a convoy from Ramrod to Hutal. So because there were no military flights scheduled to go to Hutal Maiwand until another week or so, I had to find out if contractors would go to Ramrod and if I could get on Space A. I found out there was one contractor going to Ramrod but it wasn't guaranteed. The day that I wanted to leave, the weather looked horrible. It was dusty and not even clear. But I gave it a shot and went to the contractor's ramp and put myself on the list. I waited 3 hours and the dispatcher later told me that the flight got cancelled due to weather. Right when I was about to make a phone call to have someone pick me up, I heard one soldier say that the flights might be back on. Suddenly the weather was clearing and there was no more dust. So the contractor told everyone that the flights were back on. When one helicopter came, I didn't make it to the flight because my name was almost at the bottom of the list. I was getting ready to call it quits and come back to Area A and try another day. Again, when I was going to call for somebody to pick me up, I heard the contractor announcing that there was another helicopter available to Ramrod. I knew I was going to make it on the list. I waited almost 6 hours on a dusty ramp to get to Ramrod. I was starving but I knew it was important to make it there. Once I did, Scramble told me that the new BSO would get me on a ground convoy. As I already mentioned, the BSO is the head military commander for our Area of Operations. It was my first time in Ramrod and had no idea where I was. When I left the helicopter, I didn't know where to go when a soldier that was on the flight and who got off with me asked me where I was going. I told him that I wanted to get to the transit tent and find out where the BSO was. He took me there and, once I reached it, I registered my name and asked for the point of contact for the BSO. He told me that Scramble had been in contact with them and that I was going to be able to get on a ground convoy. It was only a 15 minute ride from Ramrod to Hutal. So I finally made it to Hutal. It was a good feeling to be back after a long travel from America.

Now that I was back and with a feeling about what was going on, it was important to find out where we were. Before I left Maiwand, I told Scramble that it was important to move forward with the local NGO WP. WP would be implementing the VTC for us. During my absence, Scramble was able to work with WP on the preliminary budget numbers. We all agreed for two courses: masonry and tailoring. As I already mentioned, it was important for us to empower our Afghan colleagues and we needed the project to be vetted through DG Karimi and DDA. We didn't have any issues with DG Karimi but we were having issues with the DDA Chairman. The DDA Chairman was from Kandahar City and didn't come very often to Maiwand. We needed his support and to discuss the development projects with him. It was important to get his approval. DG Karimi didn't really care if he was present because he wanted all the projects to go around him. The DDA was in charge of coordinating the development projects. I was able to get in touch with the MRRD representatives in Kandahar City and make them aware that the DDA Chairman didn't come to the district and hadn't demonstrated interest in supporting the development efforts. The DDA falls under the leadership of the MRRD. The MRRD informed me that they would take care of it and would instruct the DDA Chairman to support the development efforts and be present whenever there was a discussion. One of the excuses the DDA Chairman gave me for not coming to Maiwand was lack of money to pay for his fuel. The MRRD told me that the DDA Chairman received a stipend and he should have been okay with the traveling form Kandahar City to Maiwand. I asked the DDA Chairman if he received money from the MRRD and he told me that he didn't. Then I told him that I'd been in touch with the MRRD and they told me that he did receive a stipend. The DDA Chairman told me that indeed he does receive some stipend but it is not enough. I asked the DDA Chairman why he wasn't honest with me. He didn't answer back and stood quiet. I told the DDA Chairman in front of DG Karimi that if he doesn't want to support the development efforts, then we needed to have a DDA Chairman that lives in Maiwand and would be always accessible. It was also important for him to take the lead at the Development Shuras and brief the elders on the current and future development activities. After our little conversation, it was all good to go. Since then, the DDA Chairman became supportive and active on all of the activities, but his involvement would have a sad finish. I will go over this later on.

Also, we had a new BSO in Maiwand and I was briefed on the new BSO objectives for Maiwand. Based on my experience, every time you get a new military unit they are pumped up to do a lot of things. I heard that they wanted to provide government housing for all the Tashkiel workers. I advised the new military counterparts that we should be careful when doing government housing because the Afghan government was having difficulty filling the Tashkiel and the workers didn't come to work. Furthermore, finding technically skilled workers to work for the government would be difficult and most likely they would have to come from Kandahar City. Eventually the military counterparts began to move forward with the so-called government housing. Later on in the year this government housing would become another empty building because it was unrealistic that the Afghan government would support the district government with Tashkiel workers.

Scramble told me the good news that an NGO expressed interest in doing a literacy course in Maiwand. This was Scramble's effort and I was happy that he took leadership to move forward with this activity. Doing a literacy course in Maiwand was important because of the high illiteracy rates in the district. I was very happy the DST started doing projects for the district. As you may recall, the first project was the radio messages, which continued through the end of my tour. The education literacy course would last for nine months and takes the student to the 3rd grade ("post-literate") level. Each grade would take approximately three months to complete. Initially, proposed classes would have 25 students and would run from 5:00 pm - 7:00 pm at a location near the main bazaar in Hutal. The students would be selected based on consultations with the Director of Education and local Shuras. The NGO announced that humanitarian assistance though food donation would be provided to the students at the literacy course. DG Karimi and DDA Chairman were happy that this project was going to be implemented for the district.

I've mentored my military counterparts but I also mentored

Scramble because he had difficulty getting adjusted to the district. I took it upon myself to mentor him and transfer my field knowledge. Scramble and I had a difficult time working with each other in the beginning. He meant well in his job but sometimes he was very negative. We lived very close to each other, so close that as soon as I opened my trailer door his trailer door was in front of mine. We had some bumps during my tour and we argued at times. I don't think he wanted to be in Maiwand in the beginning and I wanted to instill on him a sense of optimism that things were going to be okay. Scramble came to my trailer every other night and we talked for hours. He can *talk* for a period of time. Some of my colleagues sort of gave me the good luck pat on the shoulder when I told them I was working with Scramble. I didn't let that bother me because deep inside I knew he meant well and he had a good heart. Scramble was very honest and wanted to help the community. He was good at his job and our local and military colleagues and I truly appreciated it. But sometimes I had to tell him that he wasn't doing his job correctly and he took it upon himself to fix the problem quickly. I am a very disciplined person and I take my job seriously. Scramble made the effort to get to know me so we could make our jobs easier. It was important that we developed a good working relationship because our military and Afghan counterparts depended on us for all governance and reconstruction development.

I realized it was time to close the community gap that existed between the district and provincial government. When I sat with DG Karimi, I asked him about his engagement with the Line Ministry Directors. In Afghanistan, each Ministry has a Director that represents the ministry in the province. The Director (aka Line Ministry Director) oversees his ministry representatives in the district and program operations. For instance, in Kandahar Province, the Ministry of Agriculture has a Line Ministry Director of Agriculture in Kandahar City where all the Line Ministry Directors sit. Then the Line Ministry Director Agriculture would have a Maiwand District Director of Agriculture who is subject to the Line Ministry Director of Agriculture in Kandahar City. DG Karimi told me that he rarely engaged with the Line Ministry Directors. Then I told DG Karimi to not lie to me because I know he visited them every Saturday at the Governor's Palace. Then he told me, well, yes it is true that he engages with them, but his engagement doesn't have any really substance because they didn't seem to want to help out the districts. I told DG Karimi about the idea of bringing the key Line Ministry Directors to Maiwand. I understood his frustration because many Directors didn't want to come to Maiwand unless they were paid extra and would only come with a dedicated helicopter. Paying extra an Afghan government official for visiting the districts was not right. I still remember the day when DG Karimi called the Line Ministry Director of Agriculture to invite him to a meeting in Maiwand to discuss agriculture efforts. The Line Ministry Director of Agriculture told DG Karimi that he would not come to Maiwand unless he was paid an extra $250. What was amazing was that the Line Ministry Director of Agriculture was saying these things to DG Karimi on the phone while he was at a meeting with the Canadians. I told the Canadians that the response by the Line Ministry Director of Agriculture was another example of the ineffectiveness by the Afghan government.

DG Karimi told me that he wanted only the Line Ministry Directors that he believed could really help Maiwand, like the Directors from the MRRD, Economy, and Electricity. So we told him that we would facilitate the proper transportation of the Line Ministry Directors. I didn't have their contact information and DG Karimi wanted to contact them from my trailer. DG Karimi lost his cell phone and lost his primary contacts. So I told him that I would try to get the contact info from the KT team in Kandahar City. I sent emails to the KT governance unit and they told me that they would not provide me with the contact information. They told me I first needed to work around their schedule and then, if it worked for them, they would engage with the Line Ministry Directors and Deputy Provincial Governor. DG Karimi wanted to invite the Deputy Provincial Governor. I was actually ready for this answer, so I told them that it was fine. I told DG Karimi that I couldn't get the info, and DG Karimi told me that he would go again to Kandahar City and would get all the necessary info and would personally invite the Line Ministry Directors for MRRD, Economy, Electricity, and Deputy Provincial Governor. I was pleased with the effort by DG Karimi because it began to show his commitment to work in governance and be transparent. When DG Karimi returned from Kandahar City, he told me he invited them but wanted to double check with the invitees again and finalize the expected date, for the first week of June. Getting the transportation was going to be difficult because we had to get a dedicated military helicopter for an early pick up and drop off on the same day. We worked hard and we have to thank our military counterparts for making this happen. I sat with DG Karimi to discuss his strategy and the type of questions he was going to ask the Line Ministry Directors and Deputy Provincial Governor. DG Karimi wanted to make sure there was an agenda and he wanted to send his message to the provincial leadership. We sat for the rest of the month talking and discussing what the key ministries could do for him despite the fact that there was already a budget allocated and nothing was going to come downstream to the district. I advised DG Karimi that it was important to see what he could get out from the MRRD because they received a lot of funds from CIDA through the NABDP Phase III whereby he might get some assistance for reconstruction projects. He was happy I passed this information on to him and he was going to focus on MRRD projects that the ministry could do in the district. Another key player was the Director of the Economy, who also served as the Provincial Development Council (PDC) Chairman. This is a good position at the Province Level because the PDC approves the final development budgets for the district and the PDC Chairman communicated with several aid agencies in Kandahar City. We were going to bring the Director of Justice but he cancelled at the last minute because he got shot in the arm. It was sad to hear that he was shot but I was happy he didn't die. The Director of Electricity was important. DG Karimi knew he may not get anything from him but it was still important for the Director of Electricity to come to the district because one of the peoples' top complaints was the lack of electricity. Our military counterparts were very pleased with this effort because it showed that we had started with the mentorship of DG Karimi and he became more active in his role as District Governor. DG Karimi recommended having the DDA at the meeting because the DDA fell under the MRRD leadership. The meeting was broken into two parts. First, when the visitors came, they would meet in DG Karimi's office and discuss their needs and how they could assist the district. DG Karimi didn't want to jump right away into a meeting with the elders and the Line Ministry Directors because it could become very disorganized as the elders would talk and talk and never stop. Once the first part of the meeting took place at DG Karimi's office, then DG Karimi and the visitors would move to the conference room to meet with the elders to listen to their problems. I realized this meeting was becoming symbolic because something like this hadn't been done before, especially when the District Governor takes the initiative.

    Two weeks before the meeting took place, the KT requested another governance and development meeting. We just had one right before I left on R&R and they wanted another one. I didn't know how much I was going to talk about governance and development because nothing had really changed from four weeks ago. It was ridiculous that they wanted another one but they asked for it and they got it. I prepared another detailed PowerPoint presentation and spoke for almost 3.5 hours non-stop. I went over everything regarding governance and development. One of the things that came up at the meeting was the upcoming meeting we were organizing for DG Karimi to bring the key Line Ministry

Directors. The KT was shocked that we were able to move forward with the arrangements and everything was set for the Deputy Provincial Governor and other key Line Ministry Directors to come. I asked the KT to help me out and let one of our translators go to the KT base and overnight there so he could welcome the Deputy Provincial Governor and the Line Ministry Directors to the KT base in order for them to get on the helicopter. The KT Director asked me why I didn't reach out to them for their assistance. I told him that I requested their assistance but I didn't get much support and I was very upset when one of the KT staff told me by email that I had to work around his schedule first before they could contact the Line Ministry Directors. They didn't want to give me the Line Ministry Directors' contact information. I told the KT Director that I only have a one-year tour to make things happen and would not waste my time sitting around and waiting for people to help me out. So I went directly to the source to arrange the visit. No big deal. I think the KT Director was shocked at how organized we were and it demonstrated that I didn't really need KT to support me. In reality, I didn't because through the short time that I was in Maiwand, the KT demonstrated ineffectiveness in supporting us. The KT Director asked me if he was copied in the emails. I told him that I had him copied in the emails. The KT Director told me that he was too busy doing other stuff and probably hadn't had time to read my emails. Well, that wasn't my problem if people didn't want to read what we were doing. But we always kept everyone in the loop. The KT Director apologized and told me that they would support and assist me with anything we needed to do in order to make this meeting symbolic. The more hands the better, so I welcomed his support for the meeting. He asked me if he could come to the meeting and I had no objection.

For all us in Maiwand the meeting was important because it was the beginning of putting Maiwand in the spotlight again and showed people that we were turning around the district that at one point looked like it was going to collapse. The meeting was scheduled for the first week of June. The first part of the meeting took place at the District Governor's office because DG Karimi wanted to have a private meeting with the Afghan government officials to discuss in depth Maiwand's problems. The meeting then moved to the conference room where the Deputy Provincial Governor and the Line Ministry Directors met with the elders. Below was the agenda structure:

a. DG Karimi introduction – DG Karimi provided a briefed introduction on the history of Maiwand, budget request, security, education, health, and past/ongoing/future development projects.
b. Security – Ongoing confiscation of weapons. Continuing ALP recruiting efforts and training. ISAF continues with the construction of new checkpoints.
c. Education – Three new schools within the past 12 months have reopened. Provided briefed background on how many students roughly attend the school.
d. Health – Hutal Clinic continues to provide basic health services.
e. Past/ongoing/ request for future reconstruction & development projects – USAID (i.e.: refurbishment of the Hutal School, solar lights installation, canal cleaning, road rehabilitation, and retaining walls). Repairs to the new District Government Building. Construction of the Agricultural Center. Would like to receive power from the Kajaki dam. Some development projects could not be implemented in isolated villages such as Band I Timor because of the security situation and it is in Taliban control area. Possible fill the tashkiel with engineers that could work on development projects. Resource and tasks the tashkiel civil servants. The DST linkage with the Kandahar City NGOs is empowering the DDA.

For me the most important area DG Karimi touched on during his brief was the budget process and Ministry of Finance Budget pilot projects with the Ministry of Education, Health, Agriculture, and MRRD. DG Karimi indicated his desire to know the baseline costs and the proposed new activities submitted by the budget units of the respective ministry. DG Karimi showed the Director of Economy the 1391 Budget formulation. DG Karimi asked for the total development amount that would be allocated for Kandahar Province and what sub-national program could be utilized in Maiwand. We mentored DG Karimi on the budget process because the budget is the primary tool for implementing government policies and priorities. The DST informed DG Karimi that the budget units from the pilot ministries are required to align their programs structures, outputs, and indicators with the ANDS (Afghan National Development Strategy) results framework. The Deputy Provincial Governor and Director of Economy were impressed by DG Karimi's knowledge on the Afghan government budget circulation. The Director of Economy promised DG Karimi that he would assist them with the linkage with local Kandahar City NGOs and the most important surprised from the meeting was when the MRRD Director promised DG Karimi that they would use the remaining NABDP Phase III Canadians funds to do water wells and biogas projects. This offer was symbolic because for the first time we had an Afghan government official committing to do something even on a small scale in the district. I wasn't going to leave this promise hanging in the air and I knew that it was important to follow up to make sure the wells and biogas project were implemented. The MRRD also informed us about the upcoming delivery of WFP food distribution and the information was helpful to the DDA Chairman to get ready for the distribution the following month.

At the second part of the meeting the Deputy Provincial Governor and Line Ministry Directors met with key elders. The Deputy Provincial Governor congratulated DG Karimi for his outstanding presentation to explain the needs of the district. The elders were pleased with the donation of the motorcycles by the Deputy Provincial Governor. Some elders expressed dissatisfaction with the Director of Electricity because nothing has been achieved since his last trip to Maiwand last year. The Deputy Provincial Governor acknowledged the mistakes by the Afghan government with the implementation of reconstruction and development projects and promised that the Afghan government would try to fix the lack of coordination. An elder changed the pace of the meeting from development to security when he requested that his son be released. This elder's son was captured for transporting poppy. According to the elder his son was innocent. Several elders expressed their support for the release of this detainee. The elders promised to write a letter that would guarantee that the detainee would not commit another crime. The Deputy Provincial Governor mediated this issue with the District Chief of Police (DCOP). This case was solved in this meeting. However, it continues to demonstrate the need to have an active prosecutor to address detainee issues. The Deputy Provincial Governor recorded a message to express his support for the people of Maiwand. This message was played on the radio station. The Deputy Provincial Governor demonstrated enthusiasm and his attitude lived up to the expectations. The Deputy Provincial Governor closed the meeting by telling the elders to not lose hope because he would continue work for the people of Maiwand.

Overall, the meeting served its purpose to bring DG Karimi closer with the Afghan government provincial officials. DG Karimi's knowledge demonstrated his continuing commitment to improve his leadership as a leader of the District Government and to serve the needs of Maiwands. This meeting was symbolic because it demonstrated that we were building a good foundation for governance and development. It was important to have a District Government that would be able to produce sound policy making decisions, budget decisions, management, and accountability. This was a historic and symbolic meeting because we were strengthening the responsibility at the local level, enhancing transparency, and assisting in the development of a sub-national government that is capable of being self-sufficient, and capable of identifying the needs of the citizens. This was a meeting for DG Karimi to sit down with the Deputy Provincial Governor, key Line Ministry Directors and find realistic solutions that would complement the Afghan National Development Strategy 2008 - 2013.

We had an American NGO, which I call "WF." WF's main effort was to turnaround the Model Farm that was literally abandoned. As I already mentioned before, it was important to do something with the Agriculture Center, and I didn't have the real capacity and expertise to revamp it. When Team D was in Maiwand, they tried to assist with the agricultural efforts but they didn't get support from the Maiwand Director of Agriculture. The Maiwand Director of Agriculture didn't want to work unless he was paid more money despite the fact that he was already getting paid by the Afghan government, and it was under his roles and responsibilities to assist with any project that fell under agriculture. I met the WF representative and he was an ex-pat farmer with a lot of experience. For instance, one of the first things he did was training on soil preparation for crop rotation, summer cropping with minimal water usage, and subsistence farming techniques. The ex-pat farmer would do first a technical training and use one of the Agriculture Center buildings and then he would take the farmers to the Model Farm for hands-on training. The trainings were also broadcasted on our radio station. After the training, the farmers received seed and fertilizer. If you didn't give the farmers something, they would not come to the training.

Moving along with our efforts to mentor DG Karimi and the DDA on how to do development projects, as I mentioned before, it was important that we delivered a project directly to the community. I mentioned previously that we brought local NGOs to Kandahar City to discuss with elders, DG Karimi, and DDA what they wanted to do. They wanted many things like roads, vocational training classes, and assistance with health. After back and forth consultation with the U.S. Embassy on the type of projects they could fund, we came to the agreement that we would do the First Vocational Training Center in Maiwand, and we would use one of the buildings from the Agriculture Center. We submitted the proposal to the U.S. Embassy to do a masonry and tailoring class. The submission was symbolic because it wasn't only the Afghans working on the project and we as a team put a lot of effort to make this submission symbolic. It was the first time something like this was happening in Maiwand and most importantly, we were empowering our Afghan colleagues and ourselves. The fact that things looked like they were moving forward was a good sign that we were turning Maiwand around. For our new military counterparts, they were happy to see that something like this was moving forward and they wanted to assist with the project as well. We never said no to assistance, so we asked the military to help the trainees graduate. The military committed to support the graduates with micro-grants and promised to hire the masons or tailors on CERP projects. It was more likely that the military would hire masons than tailors because the military did more construction work. If we could train 15 masons and then we could find them at least short-term jobs, this was very important. We wanted to do a tailoring class because we found many tailor shops in the local bazaar and the elders and DG Karimi requested a tailoring class. We wanted to target 15 masons and 25 tailors. This Vocational Training Center (VTC) would provide opportunities for training in an area that was undergoing recovery. Our goal was to help trainees to find productive employment and become socially and economically independent. The main beneficiaries would be the villagers surrounding the Hutal Hub who were recovering from insurgent conflict. It was important to keep the youth away from violence. Vocational training in Maiwand was for a long time considered a second rate alternative. The VTC's intent was to change this perception. The 40 beneficiaries from this vocational training represented the villages of Chelgazi, Mohammad Musa Kalay, Nasu Kalay, Ata Mohammad, Moshak, Sarwar Kariz, Mazaraeh, and Pir Zadeh. In essence, the vocational training played a role to help Maiwands make the most of the employment opportunities. The VTC was set up as a pilot project to give opportunities to the young males to learn a skill and increase their chances to find non-agricultural jobs. If the VTC went well, then we would move forward with more similar projects.

One of the efforts we wanted to do and try to get it right was to take DG Karimi out of his bubble and have him engaged with the locals. People in Afghanistan didn't have faith in their government and one of the important things to do was to create this faith among the Afghan people. The Taliban takes every opportunity to overshadow the Afghan government and try to convince the local population that the Afghan government is not legitimate. Sometimes it was difficult to convince people that the Afghan government would provide public services. The Taliban created a shadow government and elected its own District Governor. The Taliban system probably brought justice quicker to the villagers. If you looked at what the Afghan government was doing regarding rule of law, nothing was moving forward. So even people who had nothing to do with the insurgent activities, they looked after the Taliban shadow rule of law system. Villagers didn't have faith in the Afghan government. Despite the fact that there was no support from the Afghan government provincial authorities, DG Karimi told me that it was still important to get out of his bubble at the District Center and visit the villagers. I praised DG Karimi for this effort because he knew the risks that came with this effort, which meant putting his life on the line at the risk of getting killed by the Taliban. It was important to not only have community meetings or Shuras at the District Center but also in the villages. The idea was to bring the government closer to the villages and listen to the District Governor. We call this effort "GIRoA Outreach Shura." GIRoA stands for "Government of the Islamic Republic of Afghanistan." We did the first GIRoA Outreach Shura in Chelgazi, which was not far from our base. Our military and Afghan counterparts provided the security for DG Karimi and DST. We decided to walk to the village and let DG Karimi conduct his Shura. It was interesting to walk around Hutal. Although I could understand that it would have been better to have only DG Karimi travel on his own with his security, at that time, looking at the security situation, the military had to provide a good portion of the security. We took a walk to the Chelgazi village. It was fascinating walking to Chelgazi because it was the first time that we were embedded walking around the neighborhoods in Hutal. The streets were very narrow and the children would surround us every step of the way. I saw a lot of poverty just by looking at the houses. There was a lot of garbage and dust. It was a very hot afternoon. The temperature was probably around 114 degrees and it felt a lot hotter with the body armor. I had to drink a lot of water because it was easy to get dehydrated. As we walked, villagers would stop DG Karimi and kiss his hands. I guess it was a sign of respect. In Chelgazi people respected DG Karimi because he was born there. We walked to the local mosque to meet a group of elders. From the mosque, all key players went to an open area for DG Karimi to hold his first GIRoA Outreach Shura. The elders brought a large rug to the open area and they all sat there. We had the presence of 30 elders. We had to take off our shoes and the elders were ready to engage with DG Karimi. We sat in the background because we wanted this meeting to be all Afghan led. The elders shared their frustration with the Afghan government for the lack of essential services especially of water. Many of the elders requested more hand water well pumps. One elder informed DG Karimi that if the lack of electricity problem was not solved, people would leave Maiwand. DG Karimi expressed sadness by the lack of services the elders had to confront on a daily basis. DG Karimi promised the elders that he would bring their complaints to the PG. DG Karimi explained to the elders that the Afghan government was broken and it was difficult to get assistance from them. The GIRoA Outreach Shura was symbolic because it is the first time a District Governor in Maiwand got outside his comfort zone. The activity proved the ability of DG Karimi to assist in the development of a sub-national government that was willing to become transparent and capable of identifying and prioritizing the needs of the villagers. The day following the Shura, DG Karimi came to the COP and requested to speak to me. It was a Thursday night and it was rare for DG Karimi to come to the COP because it was his routine to travel to Kandahar City from Thursday to Saturday. DG Karimi came straight to my trailer and wanted to talk about the GIRoA Outreach Shura. He told me that he wasn't sure how he was going to help the people in Chelgazi because he was not getting the proper support from the Afghan government to deliver public services to the villages. So we brainstormed about how we would do it. We decided to get together with my military counterparts and assist with a small project in Chelgazi. To do a small quick impact project in a village after a DG's visit would have a positive after effect. DG Karimi welcomed the idea and wanted to organize another meeting with the Chelgazi Village Leader to discuss what type of project we could do. The Chelgazi Village Leader informed DG Karimi that they wanted to do a hand water well pump. We wanted to be very careful about doing wells because the canals were drying up and villagers didn't know how to conserve the water. However, we understood that water was one of the main necessities. We decided to do only two small hand water well pumps. We actually wanted the Afghan government to build a well but we all knew that it wasn't going to happen. Actually, the Afghan government promised that they were going to do 130 wells in Maiwand. They claimed that they had done it but we could not verify it. Overall, I was pleased with the effort to take out DG Karimi outside this security bubble. As I already mentioned, it was important to start building a transparent government even if the central government didn't want to assist. Our DG did the best he could to listen and bring the people's needs to his higher-ups.

By mid June, I had begun to think about the progress that we were making. We had positive signs to show that we were on the right track. The civilian-military relationship was repaired and the DST enjoyed a good relationship with DG Karimi, DDA, and rest of the elders. By mid June, DG Karimi showed signs that he was turning the district around with the minimum resources he had at his disposal. All the efforts were now well synchronized where we were all part of the successes. There was no more talking about DG Karimi getting removed. To the contrary, there was talk on the positive job he had been doing by leading the district to good governance, transparency, and accountability. When I came to Maiwand, I was scared about the possible outcome. By June, there was no more fear, but enthusiasm to continue to work in Maiwand because we had a strong foundation for success. For the DST it was not only important to mentor our Afghan counterparts but also important to mentor our military counterparts who didn't have enough experience in economic and political development. I was pleased to see our military counterparts take greater involvement on how to address governance and development. For instance, Hola did a Water Shura, which launched again the discussion of the water problems in Maiwand. It was important that our military counterparts felt empowered to be creative in this type of work. I've always told everyone that the DST couldn't do everything and that two minds could think better than one.

Good synchronization was improving among ourselves (civil - military) and I also wanted to have good synchronization with our Afghan colleagues. It was important to know what everyone was doing so if something went wrong, we could help each other. Also, it was important to begin to empower the DDA with the coordination of development projects. At the development working group meeting, we involved all of our key players from the DST, military (Brigade TOC (Tactical Operations Center), Battalion TOC, and DAT (District Advisory Team), and Afghan counterparts such as DG Karimi and DDA. We also took the opportunity to mentor our Afghan counterparts in development projects. For the DST it was important to make sure DG Karimi and DDA had the proper knowledge, skills, and attitudes to do the job. I knew the mentorship in governance and development was not only about correcting the weaknesses; it was about upgrading and taking people forward, which is what I wanted to do with DG Karimi and the DDA. We as a team always paid attention to how our Afghan counterparts were going to move forward. For instance, in the month of June, we discussed the names of the contractors for the water wells in the village of Chelgazi. I've mentioned that after our first GIRoA Outreach Shura we were going to do to a small, quick project. We didn't back down from this promise and it was important that we stood with our promises. Afghans were not brainless and they would listen and have high expectations about what you could deliver. If you were honest with them, they would not bother you. If you continued to make promises, they would be in your face and wait for execution. Because I was involved in the project for this GIRoA Outreach Shura it was important that we delivered. We guided and mentored DG Karimi and DDA with the contractor agreement to build two hand water well pumps. The DDA updated us on the 130 water well pumps and 10 biogas projects, which would be implemented by the MRRD. So the development working group meetings demonstrated that the mentoring and development of the Afghan officials was important because it helped them gain experience, extend their skills, and create a visible system. It was important to demonstrate to our Afghan counterparts the means to achieve economic development. The development working group meeting ensured a system and process that were fair, understandable, effective, relevant, and time- (and cost-) effective. I was pleased with the engagement by our Afghan counterparts because it not only demonstrated their positive attitude to address a problem but it also demonstrated that our perseverance in mentoring our Afghan counterparts was finally paying off.

Development Working Group Continuous Cycle Meeting

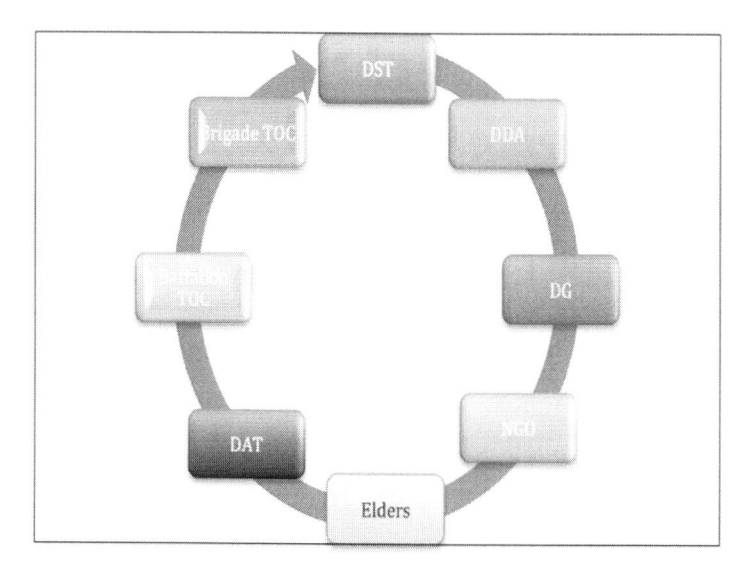

[Diagram: Circular cycle showing DST → DDA → DG → NGO → Elders → DAT → Battalion TOC → Brigade TOC → back to DST]

At the Development Shura, the DDA Chairman also briefed the elders on the projects, and he took a greater lead on the development coordination. For instance, the DDA Chairman briefed the elders not only on the 130 water wells but also on possible foreign aid assistance that was coming to Maiwand such as the WFP food distribution. When I came to Maiwand, DG Karimi wanted to do everything but slowly he began to decentralize his role to the right people. This made him a stronger leader because he began to understand that he couldn't micro-manage and do everything. It required a lot of patience working with my Afghan counterparts because I couldn't expect them to assimilate everything instantly. It takes time and you have to have the best attitude. Maiwand was a difficult and challenging environment but I always kept the best attitude that something good would come out from all the effort that we were putting into the district. As I already mentioned, Afghanistan is an infant democracy and, just like infants would make mistakes as they learned how to walk and speak, so Afghans would make mistakes as they learned how to become greater leaders and agents for their security, governance, and development efforts. This is the reason why we were there, to assist them and walk them through the process. I never wanted to impose and always tried to move strategically to what the culture and current situation would allow me. Lowering my expectations contributed to my good attitude and ability to see things in perspective. I needed the good attitude because if I didn't have it, as the lead in governance and development, then the people that surrounded me would have given up. I was able to demonstrate to my military counterparts the processes of development. They didn't believe that we could turnaround a district. And slowly they began to see the greater role that DG Karimi took in the district. For many, probably this mentorship might not seem like a lot, but when you are in rural Afghanistan where security and lack of education are major problems, the fact that our Afghan counterparts began to do something about it by speaking out was symbolic in itself.

If you remember, one of strongest efforts was to continue to close the communication gap between the provincial and district level. We had a positive outcome when we brought the Deputy Provincial Governor and other key Line Ministry Directors. Now, we were moving forward strategically with DG Karimi on rule of law. I say strategically because every step that we took had purpose.

- First, it was important to bring the key Line Ministry Directors. We did it.
- Second, before Ramadan started, it was important to push for rule of law and bring the key rule of law officials to Maiwand. Our DG wanted to send a signal that it was safe for the judicial officials to work in Maiwand. Rule of law was something that also fell in line with the Afghan national strategic plan.
- Third, during September, it was important to do media outreach to show the media that progress had been made in Maiwand.

- Fourth, after the media outreach, follow-ups would continue with the provincial authorities to make sure they didn't forget their promises to Maiwand.

Things didn't move quickly in Afghanistan and certainly it was more difficult in rural areas like Maiwand. Our efforts would serve as a foundation when new people would come to Maiwand. It was important not to reinvent the wheel and, at the DST level, we wanted to make sure the proper foundation was set in place. The governance foundation would not only be useful for a new DST but it would also be useful for our new military counterparts in the future and, if we had a new DG, then for him as well.

The rule of law meeting was going to take a lot of energy but I knew rule of law would be an important move that would set up the district as an example. I also knew that organizing another important visit would take a lot of coordination effort. We had a small team and we also assumed the administrative responsibility to make sure we had the visitor confirmation and proper military air assets. Scramble and I sweated it out. Below is what it would take to coordinate this effort:

- Talk to DG Karimi.
- DG Karimi would need to think about the effort and decide if it was important.
- Meet several times with DG Karimi to discuss the appropriate steps to move forward with the rule of law effort.
- Talk to the KT team and make them aware that we were moving forward and needed their assistance to make sure the Afghan Judicial Officials were allowed to go inside their camp to take the flight to Maiwand – Hutal.
- Convince our military counterparts so we could have the appropriate support including military dedicated air asset.
- Because the mobile network was bad in our area, we brought several times DG Karimi to our COP to call from our trailer the Afghan Judicial Officials.

- DG Karimi had to come back several times because the Afghan Judicial Officials were not picking up the phone.
- Be patient with DG Karimi and not impose on him too much to come to the base to speak with the Afghan Judicial Officials.
- We didn't have a dedicated translator, so Scramble and I always had to run around our COP to find a good translator.
- After DG Karimi spoke over the phone with the Afghan Judicial Officials, we had to double check to see that they were coming.
- Coordinate with the KT team and inform them to remind the Afghan Judicial Officials on the target date to visit Maiwand. The KT team had a weekly engagement with the Afghan Judicial Officials, so it was important they served as a reminder. I was happy to see that the KT was more active and involved in our effort. This time, they knew we were serious about making things happen for the district.
- Worked with the military to make sure we could get dedicated military flight that would bring the Afghan Judicial Officials. Getting a dedicated flight to come to Maiwand wasn't easy. I had to justify to my military counterparts the importance of the meeting. Military flights didn't come often to Maiwand so I knew that if something went wrong and the weather didn't help us out, we would have to wait for another couple of weeks. Ramadan was within a month, and I knew that if we couldn't make the meeting happen, then we would have to wait until September or later in the Fall.

We reviewed the coordinating points over and over to make sure we were all on the same page. It could be very exhausting. It would take not only good coordination among DG Karimi and us but it took a lot of communication between the Afghan Judicial Officials and DG Karimi. Convincing provincial authorities to come to Maiwand was difficult because almost everyone in Kandahar City had a vision that in Maiwand – Hutal the security was extremely dangerous. For almost the entire month of June DG

Karimi and our team met on a daily basis to go over the logistics and the topics he wanted to discuss with the Afghan Judicial Officials. DG Karimi called the Provincial Chief Judge, Attorney General, and Director of Justice to invite them to the rule of law working group meeting. DG Karimi wanted to talk about the possibility of bringing a judge and attorney general, and about having a building to house a judicial center. The interest and involvement by DG Karimi to push forward with rule of law demonstrated that he wanted to change the governance situation. Again, our mentorship continued to pay off and I was happy that I was seeing it with my own eyes. DG Karimi invited the Director of Justice to come to Maiwand and he said that he might make it to the meeting since he was still recovering from getting shot by an insurgent. Getting shot is a sad reality for many Afghan officials because the insurgents would go after them. To our luck, we had a brave Director of Justice that was willing to come to Maiwand for the meeting. This meeting was symbolic because it was the first time in Maiwand that a high-ranking Afghan Judicial Officials accepted a DG invitation to come to Maiwand. We were mentoring DG Karimi to make sure he asked for realistic promises from the Afghan Judicial Officials. DG Karimi also welcomed the mentorship because he knew that wasting time and resources was not acceptable. DG Karimi's actions not only fell under the Afghan government strategy but also under President Obama's Afghanistan-Pakistan Strategy of "Afghan First" that calls for empowering Afghan institutions and leaders to take a leading role in their country. As part of the transition vision for 2014, it was important for us at the lowest level to assist our Afghan counterparts in gaining the capacity and resources to take charge of their own future and government development.

The meeting was schedule for the first week of July. As already mentioned, the next symbolic meeting took a large significant coordination effort. We continued to have daily follow ups. DG Karimi came to the COP two days prior to the meeting to discuss the final coordination preparation. On his visit, we also took the opportunity to celebrate the 4th of July. Just as we celebrated the Afghan holidays, we invited our Afghan counterparts to our COP for a warm dinner. We tried to not to talk about work but we still discussed the upcoming rule of law meeting and the importance of the visit by the Afghan Judicial Officials in Maiwand. The weather looked good and DG Karimi called the Afghan Judicial Officials to confirm their attendance.

I got the word from the military that the flight was going to be supported and that we were good to go for July 5th. The helicopter picked up the visitors from the KT landing zone. We had a bit of a scare because there were some miscommunications when the pilots arrived at the KT landing zone. There was a change of names of the landing zones in our area of operations from English to Pashto –our base was not called anymore Rath but Hutal. But I guess the word didn't get out that quickly. So when the pilots told the visitors and expats from the KT that they were going to COP Hutal, the visitor and expats from the KT team told the pilots that they were going to COP Rath. So the visitors and expats from the KT didn't get inside the helicopter. Word of the name change got to a few members of the KT team. So when the pilots arrived in COP Hutal, they only brought two military judicial advisors. When the BSO and I greeted them, we asked where the other visitors were and they told me that they didn't know and they just got inside the helicopter. I started to freak out because once the helicopter landed in our COP, the next time they would show up to the COP would be in the afternoon to pick up the visitors. I didn't want the visitors to wait for a long time and then just give up and not come to Maiwand. So we asked the air asset team to go back to the KT and pick up the visitors. We had to wait another 35 minutes. When DG Karimi came to the COP, I told DG Karimi that now we would have less time for him to discuss his topics. I apologized for the inconvenience. DG Karimi was very flexible and knew that getting people from Kandahar City on a dedicated flight was difficult.

After 35 minutes, the visitors arrived and we all greeted them in the landing zone. We had the attendance of influential Afghan Judicial Officials that included the Provincial Chief Judge, Director of Justice, Provincial National Director of Security (NDS), and Provincial Attorney General. Aside from the Afghan visitors, we had representatives from the KT and Area A rule of law team. DG Karimi opened the meeting by thanking the Afghan Judicial Officials for coming to Maiwand to discuss rule of law. DG Karimi provided a brief summary on Maiwand's government services, development projects, security joint efforts, and the ALP program. He also pointed out the following problems related to rule of law:

- People in Maiwand are requesting more security presence in the isolated areas far from the Hutal hub.
- A dedicated attorney general would address the confusion among Maiwand's security heads on how to prosecute cases.
- DG Karimi sometimes finds himself acting as the judge and prosecutor and had difficulty mediating cases.
- DG Karimi requested more guidance on how to prosecute criminal cases.
- DG Karimi is aware that the Afghan government needs to take greater control of solving criminal and political cases. The Director Chief of Police (DCOP) and Maiwand NDS Chief sometimes are confused with the legal procedures. We all knew that Maiwand would make a significant step if it received at least a judge or a dedicated attorney general.
- Some elders continued to question the absence of a judge in Maiwand.
- DG Karimi questioned the Provincial Attorney General Representative on why Maiwand doesn't get a dedicated attorney general.
- DG Karimi stressed the importance of filling his legal Tashkiel and the District Government is ready to provide the land if a judicial center needs to be built or one of the Agriculture Center buildings could be used temporarily as a courtroom.

The Chief Judge welcomed DG Karimi's invitation to Maiwand. He appreciated DG Karimi's leadership and effort to bring the key provincial Afghan Judicial Officials to Maiwand. The Chief Judge understood DG Karimi's frustration with the lack of presence by the judge and the attorney general. It would be difficult for legal civil servants to come to Maiwand solely on an Afghan salary. Danger pay sometimes was necessary in order to provide an incentive to work in the rural districts. The Chief Judge told DG Karimi that there was a judge assigned to Maiwand and that he had an office in Kandahar City. This was the first time DG Karimi heard that there was a judge assigned to Maiwand in Kandahar City. It was interesting to find this information. If we didn't bring the Chief Judge, we would have never found out that there was actually a judge already assigned to Maiwand. We had a sitting judge, getting a salary, but doing nothing. The Chief Judge told DG Karimi that he would try get a new judge to travel to Maiwand at least once a month to discuss with the Maiwand security heads the criminal and political cases. The Chief Judge also wanted DG Karimi and Maiwand's security heads to guarantee proper security to the Afghan Judicial Officials when they travelled from Kandahar City to Maiwand. The Chief Judge had the old Afghan perception that it is dangerous to travel on Highway 1. Highway 1 was a road that connected Maiwand to Kandahar City. Maiwand's DCOP and ANA commander assured the Chief Judge that it was safe to travel along Highway 1. The DCOP offered his services to pick up the Afghan Judicial Officials from Kandahar City and escort them to Hutal. The Chief Judge recommended the construction of a local courtroom. This courtroom would be located in a neutral location close to the District Center. The Chief Judge informed DG Karimi that the Ministry of Justice had funds to build a judicial center and he could make this request to Kabul. In the meantime, DG Karimi told the Chief Judge that he would make available one of the Agriculture Center buildings for a temporary courtroom.

Following the Chief Judge's speech, the Provincial Attorney

General Representative spoke. The Provincial Attorney General requested that DG Karimi contact Maiwand's attorney general by phone if he had any questions on criminal cases. This attorney general was assigned to Arghandab and the Provincial Attorney General told DG Karimi that he would make him available to support Maiwand while he tried to find a full time dedicated attorney general. I didn't know that Maiwand *had* an attorney general. This was news to me and DG Karimi told me that there was one, but that the attorney general from Arghandab that was supposed to cover Maiwand as well never came to Maiwand unless he got more money. According to DG Karimi, Arghandab's attorney general hadn't demonstrated his commitment to prosecute cases in Maiwand. The Arghandab attorney general was present at the meeting and he refuted DG Karimi's comments and told DG Karimi that he worked on 11 cases in 1388 and didn't work on any cases in 1389 because DG Karimi didn't call him. DG Karimi told the Arghandab attorney general that if he wanted to assist with the prosecution of cases he must attend the Security and People's Shuras. The Afghan National Army (ANA) commander reassured the Provincial Attorney General that the Arghandab attorney general should feel safe driving to Hutal because the security in Maiwand had improved dramatically over the year, especially along Highway 1. The Provincial Attorney General and Chief Judge recommended that the DCOP and DG Karimi call the Arghandab attorney general and request his presence at the Security and People's Shuras. According to the Provincial Attorney General, the main problem that existed in Maiwand and all over Afghanistan was the low salary for the Afghan attorney general. Even if proper security was provided to an attorney general, he might not come to Maiwand because of the low salary. The Chief Judge supported the Provincial Attorney General comment by emphasizing the importance of the Kabul officials raising the salaries of the attorneys general. The Provincial Attorney General told DG Karimi that even in Kabul the districts are having problems filling Tashkiels with attorneys general because of the low salary. In the meantime, the Provincial Attorney General recommended that DG Karimi select a recent high school graduate to become Maiwand's attorney general and the Provincial Attorney General would make sure this person got the proper legal training. DG Karimi questioned this recommendation because many high school graduates in Maiwand probably didn't have the capacity to excel in the legal field. The Provincial Attorney General agreed with DG Karimi that an attorney general candidate must have some competency. The Attorney General Office had to lower its hiring standard from a university degree to a high school degree because of the poor education among Afghans. This is a major problem in Afghanistan with the filling of positions. Afghan civil servants would not come to a district even if you paid them more money and provided them security. There is a lack of motivation and morale among the Afghan civil servants. I've heard in districts where the civil servants get paid double, they still don't come to work. The Afghan government runs with this problem but has limited resources to fix it because of the lack of supply of competent civil servants.

The Director of Justice acknowledged the Afghan problem with low salaries and that Afghans would not be interested in working for the government for a low salary. Competent Afghans would prefer to work as an interpreter or with an international organization because they would make more money. If Maiwand wanted a judge, a secure location needed to be identified for the judge to work and live. DG Karimi promised that he would provide temporary housing in the District Center for the judge. The Provincial NDS Chief provided some brief guidance on how to deal with political cases, such as how long a person needs to be detained in the absence of complete evidence.

After the brief engagement between the Afghan Judicial Officials, DG Karimi, and the ANSF forces, the Afghan Judicial Officials moved to the conference room to engage with the elders. The elders welcomed the presence of the Afghan Judicial Officials because it was the first time they had visited Maiwand. One elder expressed the importance of building a judicial center because it would provide credibility to the Afghan government. The Chief Judge stressed the importance of filling the legal Tashkiel but also admitted that the Afghan government currently faced hiring problems due to low salaries. Also, the perceptions of security for the past 4 to 5 years led to the lack of staffing for judicial positions. DG Karimi knew that one of his responsibilities was to ensure that there was proper security in place. Having a functioning judicial center in place would ultimately improve the peace process. Establishing good security was the job of the entire community. Another elder told the Chief Judge that Afghan officials should feel secure coming to Hutal.

Overall, it was a good engagement between the elders and the Afghan Judicial Officials. Following the engagement with the elders, DG Karimi invited the Afghan Judicial Officials to walk to the proposed site of the temporary judicial center. The Afghan Judicial Officials were impressed with the Agriculture Center buildings. The Chief Judge told DG Karimi that the Agriculture Center could provide a short-term solution and house a courtroom. DG Karimi told the Chief Judge that he had received the support from the Deputy Provincial Governor to use the Agriculture Center building for vocational training and a judicial center. The Chief Judge promised DG Karimi that he would discuss the utilization of the Agriculture Center buildings with the PG. The meeting served its purpose to close the communication gap between the District Government and the Afghan government. This was the first meeting of its kind that took place in Maiwand with regards to rule of law. DG Karimi expressed his gratitude to the DST and the BSO for their continued support of the District Government. This rule of law effort was extremely important to everyone and we continued to do the follow-ups in the fall.

Following the successful judicial rule of law working group meeting, the only thing we had left to do was to follow up with the upcoming vocational training. We knew that Ramadan was around the corner and our Afghan NGO partner assured me that the project would continue to move forward. We also had a food distribution coming to the district with much hype because the people were looking forward to receiving the food. I couldn't believe how time went by so quickly; it was already time for my next R&R. I knew the beginning of Ramadan was going to be slow and it was the right time to take R&R. I told Scramble that it was important that we move forward with the VTC and that was my task for him. I literally told him to make it happen with no excuses. A lot of the administrative paperwork was already completed and the only thing left was for WP to launch the program. Launching the program would require a large, significant effort from Scramble to make sure all the key players were aware of the upcoming ceremony, materials were purchased, and that the trainees attended the training. We had something big coming up and as you read already, the VTC was part of our strategic plan to empower our local Afghan counterparts. So I left the control and management of the DST to Scramble.

I would have another crazy anecdote leaving Maiwand for my second R&R. Since we didn't have air support at the COP to leave Maiwand. I decided to travel to the nearest large base, Ramrod, to get out of Maiwand. I put a manifest (military flight request) in for a Thursday hoping that it would get supported. I left Maiwand on Wednesday in a military convoy and I overnighted in Ramrod at the transit tent. The BSO offered to provide me the VIP trailer but I declined it and decided to stay at the same place where all transit folks stayed. My military counterparts were surprised to hear that I wanted to stay with the rest. I guess I earned more of their respect. I didn't care and I slept on a mattress on the floor. Everything looked fine and I went at 6:00 pm to check on the flight schedule when it came out the night before. The flight looked good and they told me that I would be good to go for the next morning, leaving around 7:00 am. So this meant that I had to be at the flight line around 5:45 am. No big deal, I was happy that I was leaving soon and that I was on my way out for my second R&R. The next morning, I went to the flight line. Guess what? The military flight that I was supposed to be on got delayed due to weather back in KAF. So I asked the person in charge of the flight if they expected the flight to come to Ramrod. He said yes and we were told to wait one hour, then another hour, then another hour. After three hours of waiting, he told me that the flight got cancelled. I was very upset because that meant that I would have to stay in Ramrod for another two days or so before I could get on another flight on Space A. Otherwise I would have to say goodbye to my R&R. So after he said that the flight got cancelled, I asked the flight person if another flight was supposed to come in and he told me that no flights were scheduled for the rest of the day. The skies looked bright and sunny at our base so I knew that this weather hold in KAF would not last for a long time. I walked in a 114 Fahrenheit Degree heat back to the transit tent. When I left the transit trailer, I was headed towards the MWR to check my email. I couldn't because there was a blackout. I was a bit disappointed and I decided to walk back to the transit tent. As I walked by the transit tent, I saw helicopters getting close to the base. I stood in the middle of the road and waited to see what the helicopters were going to do and then I saw helicopter contractors getting ready to land. I quickly ran to the transit tent. I put on my bulletproof vest, took all my gear, and literally ran about a mile to the flight line zone. As I continued to run, I could see the three helicopters landing on the flight line zone. I kept running and waving to not leave yet. I was getting exhausted with all the weight I was carrying. I saw people getting on the plane and I kept waving to not leave yet. I was sweating a lot and was running out of breath. As I got to the flight line zone, it looked like there was no more space and the helicopters were ready to leave. I told the flight line zone operator that I was waiting all morning for the flight. I was literally begging that it was important that I leave. I saw one guy who appeared to be the last one they were going to allow to get on the helicopters. I was with my gear and looked disappointed that I wasn't going to make it. One of the pilots looked at me and got out of the helicopter. The pilot went to the back of the helicopter to check if there is one more seat available. Sometimes people put their bags on a seat and didn't want to make it available. Don't ask me why because I think is stupid but there are people like that. I saw the pilot moving stuff and people around and pointed at me with thumbs up that I was good to go. So I went to the helicopter with almost no breath and my mouth dry as hell. I didn't drink a lot of water the day before so I began to dehydrate. But as soon as I got into the helicopter, it was all good because I knew I was going to go home for my R&R. After a 10 minute ride on the helicopter, I landed in KAF. I waited in Area A for three days before I left on my R&R to America.

Entrance to DG Karimi's building, where it was my second home after the COP.

DG Karimi and Chief Judge walking to the COP after the first judicial visit to Maiwand.

DG Karimi explaining to the Provincial Deputy Governor and Line Ministry Directors Maiwand's problems.

GIRoA Outreach Shura in Chelgazi with DG Karimi and the villagers.

DG Karimi finally reaching out to the local populace and earning the respect among the villagers.

The children would always surround us every time we went out of the base.

The poppy fields in Maiwand.

Behind me is the old British Fort.

Celebrating 4th of July with my Afghan counterparts (DG, ALP Commander, NDS, and DCOP).

DG Karimi active listening to the villager's concern on the Taliban activities in his village.

The U.S. Army Blackhawk helicopters landing in our base to pick up the Afghan Government Official visitors.

Food donation to the literacy class

V

THE LAST PUSH

I planned my second R&R with the hope that nothing much was going to happen during my absence because Ramadan would hit the month of August. As I already mentioned, the only thing that I left for Scramble to do was to start the VTC. After a two-week break, I got back to Area A in the second week of August. I checked in with Scramble and he didn't give me good news. He told me to sit down because what he was about to tell me was going to make me hit the roof. I sat down and Scramble told me that the DDA Chairman and Clerk got arrested and they were in jail. That was a complete shock to me. I didn't have words and I still had a hard time understanding what went wrong. The World Food Program (WFP) did a food distribution and apparently it didn't go well. The DDA Chairman and Clerk got arrested for trying to steal the WFP food. This incident really shook the district and put a negative spotlight on DG Karimi and on all the good governance efforts we were trying to do. I wasn't in the district yet and there wasn't much I could do. I spoke with my Director and he told me that something bad had happened in Maiwand and that I need to go there to fix things. I tried to arrange an earlier flight that would take me sooner but I had to wait before I got on a helicopter to Maiwand. I couldn't do much from Area A and I wasn't getting good feedback from Scramble regarding the WFP food distribution. We were putting so much effort towards empowering our local Afghan counterparts, so hearing that the DDA Chairman and Clerk got arrested was a small setback to everyone's effort. After 4 days of trying to get back to Maiwand, I was able to get on a helicopter and landed in Maiwand the third week of August. It was Ramadan and I was hoping that things might be a bit slow so we could focus on the VTC but, unfortunately, the WFP food distribution kept everyone busy. The only good news I received was that we started the VTC as scheduled. Scramble told me that the training was going well and that was encouraging.

When I got to Maiwand, I needed to talk to my military and Afghan counterparts and find out what had really happened. The last thing I wanted was for people to jump to conclusions and start making false accusations. For me it was important to calm people's emotions. WFP planned to do a food distribution in Maiwand through the Food for Work program. Under the Food for Work program, you cleaned the canal and instead of getting paid with money you got food. The canals covered several areas including some Taliban control areas. We couldn't verify this work and it was an all-WFP led effort; we didn't interfere. The only thing that I was tracking before I left on my R&R was that through the MRRD the DDA was going to coordinate the WFP food distribution with the villagers. According to what I heard, some villagers who worked on cleaning the canals came from Taliban control areas like Band I Timor. Villagers from Band I Timor didn't want to be seen carrying sacks of wheat donated by WFP. The villagers knew that bringing food provided by WFP could put them on harm's way since the Taliban controlled that area. For this reason, the villagers from Band I Timor asked if they could store their food in the DDA Clerk's house. The DDA Clerk's house was closer to Band I Timor and the villagers could come to the DDA Clerk's house and exchange them for regular food sacks so they can go low profile.

DG Karimi was very upset with the arrest of the DDA Chairman and Clerk. Rumors began to spread that it was the Americans who were responsible for that arrest and that I had the power to release the DDA Chairman and Clerk. One thing about Afghans is that they thought just because I worked for the State Department I could vouch for the release of the DDA Chairman and Clerk. When DG Karimi found out that I was back on the COP, he came to the COP to speak to me on the DDA Chairman and Clerk and asked me if I could release them. I told DG Karimi that it was the Afghan Government who arrested them and that I would respect what the Afghan government decided. As I began to gather information, I found out the reports that the ANP wrote on the WFP case were not accurate and the distribution numbers didn't match. So I knew there was going to be a lot to cover. I got in touch with WFP and wanted to find out the actual numbers that were delivered. I confirmed that a lot of the information that was being reported was not accurate. It was important to not jump to conclusions because we didn't know the truth. The food that was sitting at the DDA Clerk's house when he was arrested was brought back to the Old District Center. The Old District Center was the point of distribution for the food. Many elders asked me to release the DDA Chairman and Clerk. I told the elders that the food distribution was done by WFP and we didn't have anything to do with the arrest nor did we have the power to release them. It was important to show respect for the sovereign state and not impose on how they should proceed with the due process. The elders respected my sincerity and requested WFP to get the DDA Chairman and Clerk released.

I advised DG Karimi that it was important that they support the last food distribution. Our military counterparts reported that some of the food was being sold at the local bazaar. I wasn't surprised. It was up to the villagers to decide what to do once they received the food. I sent an email to my superiors asking them to be patient and to let me work on the problem because too many reports were written with information that wasn't accurate. There was a rumor that the DDA members were going to boycott the Development Shura until the DDA Chairman and Clerk were released. Certainly a boycott was not something that I was looking forward to because it would look like a setback to all the governance and development efforts. It was important that the

DDA, as the new Afghan entity on development, continue to support the development efforts. The night before the next Development Shura, I requested a meeting with DG Karimi. DG Karimi and I spoke about the situation again and he couldn't guarantee me that the DDA members were not going to boycott the next Development Shura. I tried to convince DG Karimi that it was important that we continue to work on the development efforts and to let the Afghan system continue to handle the situation. DG Karimi again asked me if I could released the DDA Chairman and Clerk and I told him that I didn't have the power and that the arrest was made by the ANP. I kept telling DG Karimi that WFP did the distribution and we had nothing to do with the WFP program. All we could do is to communicate his concerns to the WFP representatives in Kandahar Province.

I knew I was going to have a long Development Shura and people would look to me for answers to solve this problem. The night before the Development Shura I did a lot of thinking and I prepared myself on how I should respond to the elders and DDA members. I knew they would be upset and would ask me to release the DDA Chairman and Clerk. The night before the Development Shura, I received an email from WFP informing me that they would send two local staff representatives to speak with the elders and they would answer their concerns. I knew that it was important that I calm everyone and that boycotting the Development Shura was not the best option. I was a bit worried and I knew every single word that would come out of my mouth should be direct, simple, and honest. I couldn't sleep the entire night just thinking about the possible reactions. I was the primary spokesperson for our *mission* in my district and I knew I had to be very diplomatic in this situation. When you are put in this type of situation, you have to bring the best out of yourself to make sure you perform well. The entire food distribution problem reached Washington and I wanted to make sure that we solved it. The district was in the path of recovery and certainly this food distribution put a negative stamp on the district.

It was August 24th a Wednesday the day of the Development Shura. At this Shura, all DDA members, DG Karimi, and elders were present. I knew the main topic of conversation would be the arrest of the DDA Chairman and Clerk. I was ready for anything despite the fact that we had no involvement and it was all WFP's problem, the community look up to us for answers. DG Karimi did his usual introduction and welcomed everyone including the WFP local staff representatives. DG Karimi didn't waste time and began to talk about the recent arrest of the DDA Chairman and Clerk. DG Karimi wasn't happy with the arrest and requested the military or the DST to help him to get the DDA Chairman and the Clerk out of jail. Both the DDA Chairman and Clerk were arrested in Maiwand and transferred right away to a Kandahar City jail. DG Karimi didn't even bother to question the ANP who arrested the DDA Chairman and Clerk. Soon, we had a couple of elders standing up and talking about the DDA Chairman's innocence. This was expected. After a couple of elders vouched for the DDA Chairman and Clerk to be released, DG Karimi turned to me and asked me what I was going to do to get them out of jail. The Shura was pack with people and there were people outside the room just waiting to hear what I was going to say. I stood up in front of everybody and I paused for a second. I took a quick look at everyone's faces and eyes and I could see anger for the arrest of the DDA Chairman and Clerk. First of all, I told everyone that I was saddened to hear that the DDA Chairman and Clerk got arrested and that both were friends of mine. I stressed the importance of letting the due process continue and that both men were under Afghan custody and not under ISAF custody. I told the elders that the food distribution was done under the WFP program and that we had no involvement with the distribution. If there were any issues, the elders and DG Karimi must engage with the two WFP local staff representatives. I pointed out to the elders that two WFP local staff representatives were present at the Shura and they could answer any questions. The elders continued to ask me to release the DDA Chairman and Clerk. I kept telling everyone that we had no involvement with the distribution and they must talk to WFP. I asked the two WFP local staff representatives to talk to the elders. The two WFP local staff representatives provided details on the distribution and how it was done and went no further to discuss the arrest. They were of no help during the Shura. After a long talk with the elders, DG Karimi finally was able to understand that he must engage with the Afghan authorities to figure out what would happen to the DDA Chairman and Clerk.

After the Shura, the two WFP local staff representatives spoke with me. I asked the WFP local staff representatives what the arrest was all about. I wanted to make sure there wasn't any type of miscommunication that led to the arrest. The two WFP local staff representatives informed to me that they were aware that some of the food that was stored at the Old District Center was going to be transferred to the DDA Clerk's house so villagers from areas controlled by the Taliban could pick it up. The two WFP local staff representatives told me that the villagers had the right to decide on how and where they wanted the food to be transferred. The two WFP local staff representatives gave permission to the DDA Chairman and Clerk. So they went ahead and transferred some of the food from the Old District Center to the DDA Clerk's house. According to a rumor, somebody wasn't happy with what they received and told the ANP that the WFP food was stored in the DDA Clerk's house. The ANP went there and found all the food. The ANP charged the DDA Chairman and Clerk with theft and put them in jail right away. The two WFP local staff representatives told me that the villagers already worked cleaning the canals and there was nothing wrong by transferring the food to the DDA Clerk's house so the villagers could pick it up from there. The arrest was made by the ANP and I asked the two WFP local staff representatives why they didn't tell the ANP that everything was a miscommunication. The two WFP local staff representatives didn't give me an answer. I wasn't happy. I didn't know if the two WFP local staff representatives were telling me the truth. I didn't know if DG Karimi and key elders were telling the truth as well. I didn't trust anybody because I knew something went wrong and there was probably a deal or someone got a cut that was probably not happy with it and there was a whistle blower. Getting the DDA Chairman and Clerk released could've been an easy case because the only thing that was needed was for WFP to admit that they gave permission to transfer the food from the Old District Center to the DDA Clerk's house.

Now the question was what to do with the food that was found at the DDA Clerk's house. There was a good quantity left, and it was brought back to the Old District Center. The two WFP officers told me that they had talked to the DDA members and DG Karimi and decided to distribute this food in the last week of August. The distribution would take place in the morning with the presence of WFP officers, DG Karimi, and DDA members. WFP invited me to attend the distribution but I declined. This was a WFP distribution and I had no business being present during the distribution. It wasn't my program.

I emailed my superiors and the USAID folks in Washington (because there were folks already involved and tracking this case) on the upcoming distribution of the remaining food. I told them that the remaining distribution would take place at the Old District Center and that WFP would send a report on what has been distributed. I also informed everyone that there was probably a miscommunication during the distribution and that it was up to WFP to take the lead and try to fix this problem. On the day of the distribution of the remaining food, the WFP local staff representatives called me early in the morning informing me that they have arrived and would start the distribution. The distribution took the entire day and ended around 4:00 pm. The WFP local staff representatives sent me a report on what they distributed and I was happy that it went well and was transparent. When I spoke to

DG Karimi, he was in good spirits that this distribution went well. I was also in good spirits because finally we made a good distribution, but it took a lot of coordination and leadership to make sure it was transparent.

Overall, the WFP food distribution represented a small setback for the district. Doing development work in the field was very difficult and it was *OK* to have setbacks. I always tried to look at the lessons learned and it was important that we all moved forward. Many of us in Maiwand were critical about WFP because we, the folks on the ground, had to answer the questions for their mistakes and mishandling of their program. I thanked the WFP local staff representatives for their support and cooperation in addressing this matter. But it was good that we were there to address the matter and hear the villager's complaints. It was important for us as a team to transmit the people's concerns to WFP in order for WFP to take the appropriate matter under control. My biggest fear was that the WFP episode was going to put a negative stamp on the district and our governance efforts. And that Maiwand would be remembered only for the WFP episode. It was important to demonstrate to the Kandahar Provincial Authorities that Maiwand was improving.

Building an infant democracy, especially in rural Afghanistan, was not easy. It was expected that we would have setbacks but this was why we were there as governance advisors, to mentor our Afghan counterparts and walk them through their mistakes. Everyone learned from the WFP episode and we wanted to continue to move forward. DG Karimi promised me that he would not allow a boycott of the Development Shura and that he would continue to support the development efforts. The key tribal elders came to my base, shook my hand and expressed their support for the development efforts in Maiwand. We were all concerned about the DDA Chairman and Clerk arrest but it was important that we continued to empower the DDA in order to continue to support the development efforts. The DST and military had a lot of projects coming to the district and without the proper support from DG Karimi and the DDA we could not fund projects. Not funding projects would negatively impact the Maiwand people. DG Karimi also knew that he was being watched by the Kandahar PG and that it was important that he demonstrated leadership to overcome the WFP setback. Before the WFP distribution we were on a roll. I knew elders would continue to ask me to get the DDA Chairman and Clerk out of jail and that was something that I was willing to tolerate. I knew at some point they would give up and everyone would move on. All I can tell you is that at the end of my tour, the DDA Chairman and Clerk were still in jail.

When I came back from R&R, we had something good going. Scramble was able to push forward with the VTC and we had the opening ceremony the first week of August. At the ceremony we still had the presence of the DDA Chairman as it was important to show that the DDA was there to support the VTC. His arrest took place the week after and that would be the last time the DDA Chairman would be in Maiwand. The ceremony was a symbolic event in Maiwand because this activity was the first of its kind. It was symbolic for the following reasons:

- We got a local Kandahar City NGO to implement the project.
- DG Karimi and the DDA worked together to select the project and trainees.
- The elders selected the trainees and villages.
- It was the first time a community came together to do a project.
- The project complemented Maiwand's Five Year District Development Plan and National Development Strategy.
- Afghans took the lead on this project.
- Project had sustainability because the trainees would be linked to other projects related to their new specialty skill.

The VTC took a lot of effort and coordination. As I already

mentioned, when I came to Maiwand there wasn't much going on in the district related to development. The DST didn't do a project directly and we didn't have a civil society. We didn't have local NGOs because they were located in Kandahar City. I mentioned before that the local NGOs in Kandahar City had a perception of Maiwand as insecure, which deterred them from coming to the district. When we organized the NGO meeting, only 5 out of 29 NGOs that we invited came to the meeting. They didn't express any interest to work in Maiwand. I knew that if I got at least only one NGO to be interested and we could do a project, more NGOs would come to Maiwand. WP was the only NGO that believed in Maiwand and we did the VTC project with them. I was happy to have WP's involvement and we were able to push forward the project to provide tailoring and masonry training. The VTC lasted for three months, with two months masonry and three months tailoring, totaling 40 trainees. We wanted to start the project small and see what the outputs would be. If it was successful then we could do another project on a large scale. It was important to progress gradually and not jump quickly into doing something with no real substance. Everything that we did highlighted our four Community Learning and Development Approaches:

a. Empowerment – Increase the ability to DG Karimi, DDA, and community villagers.
b. Participation – DG Karimi, DDA, WP, and villagers have taken part in the decision making progress.
c. Self-determination – Support the right of the villagers to make their own choices.
d. Partnership – Recognize the Afghan government, ISAF, Community, and the DST could contribute to community learning and development, and are working together to make the most of the resources available and be as effective as possible.

But the project also hinted the importance of increasing the participation of the local government, which would provide greater governance. Below is the structure the DST followed to increase the participation of the local government.

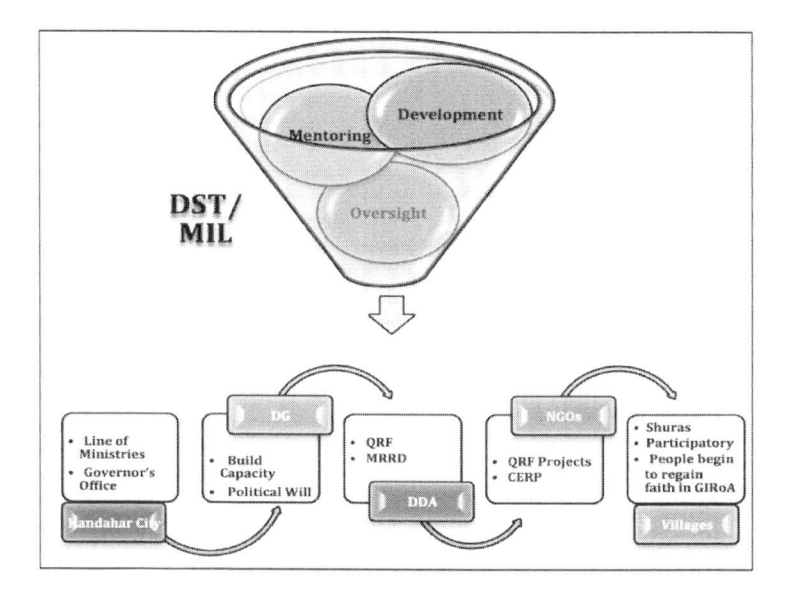

```
           ┌─────────────────────────────────┐
           │      Mentoring  Development      │
   DST/    │                                  │
   MIL     │           Oversight              │
           └─────────────────────────────────┘
                          ⬇

• Line of        ┌─DG─┐     • QRF      ┌─NGOs─┐    • Shuras
  Ministries     • Build    • MRRD                 • Participatory
• Governor's       Capacity            • QRF Projects • People begin
  Office         • Political Will      • CERP         to regain
                                                      faith in GIRoA
 Kandahar City              DDA                      Villages
```

Looking at the funnel dimensions of mentoring, oversight, and development, they all fed the VTC effort. The Kandahar City Line Ministry Director of Economy supported us to bring the NGOs, then DG Karimi pushed forward with this support to welcome the NGOs, then the DST wrote the U.S. Embassy grant in collaboration with the DDA, and then the NGO submitted the grant to the Embassy. The elders were involved with the project by selecting the villages and trainees, making the participation greater. Everything that we did as a team had a strategic purpose. The VTC took place in the Agriculture Center and the District Center. At the Agriculture Center the masons had their technical class and then went around the District Center to fix the infrastructure. The masons' first project was to build a noise generator wall at the District Police Center. After the noise generator wall, they built the entrance of the DG's building, fixed the bathrooms, built a composting pit wall at the model farm, and concluded with the generator foundation. We had 15 masons and they were excellent. They came to work every day and showed enthusiasm for learning masonry. Masonry students learned sand/cement/water mixtures, basic measures, and tool usage. Having strong on-site supervision led to changes in concrete mixture ratios, thus leading to greater load bearing capacity. Each project emphasized a specific skill set progression that focused on local needs and market conditions. Every now and then, I would bring humanitarian assistance supplies to the masons, like soccer balls or school bags, so they could provide it to their children. Scramble and I visited the masons every day and did a close monitoring. For instance, one day, I found out after talking to the trainer that he wasn't getting paid his entire salary, and the project manager was paying him less. The trainees were not getting paid their daily per diem. If it wasn't for Scramble and I always talking to the trainees and trainers to find out if everything was okay, I would have never found out about this problem. It was simple to figure out: some Afghans working directly for the WP wanted to keep this money. WP's excuse was that they had to purchase extra materials not covered under the budget, and to cover the extra expense they had to reduce the payment of the salaries. This is an old trick and I didn't buy it. I told WP that I would not tolerate corruption and if they would not spend the money according to the budget then I had no issue cancelling the project. WP promised me that it would not happen again and that the people that didn't get paid would get paid. The masons' training took place every morning from 7:00 am to 9:00 am. Scramble and I always went in the morning to observe the trainees.

I think our military counterparts really appreciated the hard effort that we put into the project. We couldn't walk on our own outside the base and we always had to be escorted by our military counterparts. Every night Scramble and I walked around the base asking them to help us out and asked them if we could tag along if they walked to the District Center. They never had an issue and they were always there, ready to help us out.

The tailoring training classes took place in the morning from 9:00 am to 11:00 am for the month of August and the early part of September. After the first week of September the classes moved to the afternoon because the children had to go to school. The focus was on teaching basic literacy and measurements, which was integral for being able to read schematics and design patterns. Tailoring students learned how to mark cloth, to measure inseams, and basic stitching. We had 25 children and the classes took place at the Agriculture Center. We bought the sewing machines, cloth, and provided all the necessary equipment to run a tailoring class. We had two trainers. It was the most exciting training course that I've ever seen. The children were always motivated to go to the classes and see Scramble and I when we came to the class. We conducted the training for three months. The first part of the month the children spend the time learning techniques. The second and third month the children began to use their new skills. For instance, the children made Afghan flags that decorated the District Center, local bazaar and 14 ANP checkpoints, and some of us purchased the Afghan flags from the children. Some of our military counterparts brought their clothes and the children fixed them. Scramble and I visited the children every morning and then later every afternoon.

Just like we provided humanitarian assistance to the masons we also provided humanitarian assistance to our tailors. All of the supplies were donated by our PSYOPS team and we didn't have words to thank them. We also ran into a problem with WP because they were not paying the children the per diem. Again, I told WP that I would cancel the project if they didn't spend the money according to the budget. There were times that I would just give up because I felt I had to be on top of everything and every single item that WP was spending. Otherwise, I could see the money disappearing. I instructed WP to make the weekly per diem payments in front of me. I counted the money, as I wanted to make sure that it was being spent properly. I didn't trust the program manager and supervisor. One thing that I knew for sure was that I wasn't going to do another project with WP.

Our military counterparts were fantastic partners for us. Samsung, who replaced Hola, was also an integral part of our success because he was very supportive and was a friend, always ready to support our development efforts. Samsung enjoyed his afternoon naps and sometimes I felt bad when I asked him for a favor to escort Scramble and I to the VTC to see the trainees. Samsung never said no and was always kind to escort us. I felt very good about the work team effort that we had in our COP among my military counterparts. They were always supportive of the DST, which is something that was absent when I first came to Maiwand. Our BSO promised that he would support our graduates who successfully completed the curriculum with CERP micro-grants. This ongoing support helped to meet the desired end state of developing a "skilled labor pool" which could be utilized for revitalization projects and/or for enhancing the pool of small-scale entrepreneurs. I can't say enough about our military counterparts on how helpful they were with our governance and development efforts. If it wasn't for them, we couldn't have achieved the VTC success.

By August time frame it was important to demonstrate what have we had gained in governance, if any, since February. I knew we were moving forward and made some progress despite the fact that we had the WFP setback with the arrest of the DDA Chairman and Clerk. Below is the update I provided on how we were moving forward. I didn't have any tools to track our progress and I took the initiative to use this one.

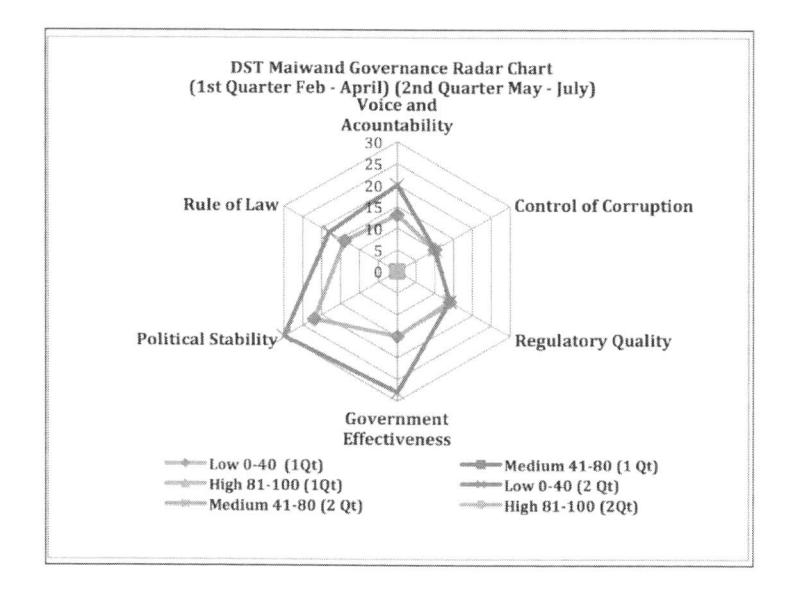

**DST Maiwand Governance Radar Chart
(1st Quarter Feb - April) (2nd Quarter May - July)**

Axes: Voice and Acountability, Control of Corruption, Regulatory Quality, Government Effectiveness, Political Stability, Rule of Law

Legend: Low 0-40 (1Qt); Medium 41-80 (1 Qt); High 81-100 (1Qt); Low 0-40 (2 Qt); Medium 41-80 (2 Qt); High 81-100 (2Qt)

Voice and Accountability – Local participation at the Development and People's Shuras continues to increase in small increment gradual levels. At the Development Shura the local population continues to interact with the DDA members on what type of reconstruction projects the Afghan government has for 1390. Thanks to the leadership by DG Karimi, the DDA Chairman has kept the locals inform on the type of projects the Afghan government or international organizations are doing in Maiwand. For this reason, locals' attendance has increased at the Development Shuras. Elders have expressed their frustration with the Afghan government during the PG's visit (April 2011), the June 7th governance working group meeting (Deputy Provincial Governor and important Line Ministry Directors came to Maiwand), and the July 5th rule of law working group meeting (for the first time key provincial Afghan Judicial Officials engaged with the district government in Maiwand). The local RIAB messages are receiving good feedback and district government officials such as DG Karimi are very supportive of putting messages on the RIAB station.

Political Stability – The District Government continues to be more stable than previous years. The Hutal areas is becoming more stable; therefore, limiting the possibility of any type of civil unrest among the local population. Although the local population may perceived the district government as a failure due to the ineffectiveness to provide 100% essential basic services, the local population appears to continue to try to work with the district government. This perception is more representative in the villages that surround the Hutal area. As you go further outside the Hutal area such as Band I Timor, this perception might change where violent means can be use to destabilized the district.

Government Effectiveness – The increase of this dimension is partly due to the reactivation of the District Development Assembly (DDA). Today, the DDA continues to show progress and it has become a tool for the local population to bring their concerns to the Kandahar Officials. The DDA Chairman has a good relationship with the MRRD officials and the MRRD has finally heard the local population complaints. The MRRD is implementing 130 hand water well pumps and 10 biogas projects. This is all Afghan-led. Although, the size of the project might not appear significant comparing to Kabul standards, the fact that the Minister of the MRRD took notice on Maiwand and they are implementing projects in the district is symbolic in itself. This is another positive outcome from the meeting we organized back on June 7th. The DST has been working behind the scenes with the DDA with the mentoring and capacity building of the DDA members. The MRRD thanked the DST for its efforts to build the capacity of the DDA members and of DG Karimi.

Regulatory Quality – This dimension is applicable more to the provincial level. However, we haven't seen any national policy that would impact the district yet. Therefore, there hasn't been any change in this dimension.

Rule of Law – We have an increase in this dimension partly because of the successful July 5th rule of law working group meeting. At this meeting, we congregated all the key provincial key Afghan Judicial Officials in Maiwand to discuss rule of law issues. It is the DST Maiwand's vision to not organize a meeting without positive outcomes and follow-ups. Similar to the positive outcomes that we had with the June 7th meeting, today, Maiwand has a part-time attorney general.

Control of Corruption – Corruption in Maiwand is inherently a difficulty reality to measure. We don't have objective indicators and we can only make subjective indicators. Nevertheless, with objective and subjective indicators we are still referring to perception-based indicators. Subjective indicators would be the frustration among locals on whether the district government is corrupt to objective data gathered from real experiences. For Maiwand it is unanimously acknowledged that perception matters with regard to corruption. However, perception is not enough and we don't have the real data as of yet to determine about actual corruption from actors involved in corruption and governance issues. We don't have the ability to obtain this information. Therefore, we can't determine whether the corruption level in Maiwand has increased or decreased. Statistically, the margin of error and level of confidence for Maiwand's corruption level will be very uneven in relation to the perception. Corruption assessment is a complicated task subject to several difficulties such as lack of objective data, and the error of measurement both endogenous and exogenous to corruption.

Overall, the DST Maiwand governance radar chart presents aggregate views on the quality of Maiwand's local government. We concluded that since February we are continuing to see a gradual improvement at the sub-national government level. This is an important step for good governance in Maiwand. There has been progress with voice accountability, political stability and absence of violence, government effectiveness, and rule of law. We have no dimension movement for regulatory quality and control of corruption. Please note that this representation is only subjective based on engagement and observations. Although this representation may not present the actual government condition, it can assist policymakers to get a snapshot on the conditions in Maiwand. I shared this information with DG Karimi and he agreed with progress.

A lot of things happened in August and, as Ramadan was coming to an end, it was going to get busier. As I mentioned before, as part of our strategy to continue to build the local government, it was time to demonstrate the progress the district had made to the local media. From the beginning of the year we started to implement small projects that were worth showing to the media. We called this event a "GIRoA media outreach day." On this day, DG Karimi would have the opportunity to talk to the media and describe the governance and development progress. First, we brought the key Line Ministry Directors to focus on development; second, we brought the key Afghan Judicial Officials to get a start with the rule of law effort; and third, we wanted to bring the media to promote Maiwand's governance and development efforts. Putting Maiwand on the press was important in order to erase Kandahari's perception that Maiwand was an unstable district and that it was not secure. Similar to the first two events that we did, this event would require a large significant amount of coordination and communication with the Kandahar Media Press. We sat as a team with DG Karimi and he was pleased with the idea. Actually, it was mostly DG Karimi's idea because he told me that it would not be a bad idea to bring the media to the district so he could talk to them about the projects that he is doing with the Afghan government, military, and DST. We would play a key role to bring the media from Kandahar City to Maiwand. The reporters didn't want to come by car, only by air. I had to work on the air logistics. Thanks to a good friend from the KT in Kandahar City, a New York Times reporter expressed interest to come to

Maiwand and cover the district. When I heard about this possibility I jumped for joy. Having the New York Times coming to the district to cover media day would make the event more symbolic. The other reporter represented the local media from Kandahar City, which included the radio, newspaper, and television. DG Karimi invited all the Kandahar City media and he came to my trailer and issued the invitation over the phone. We had experience doing events so it wasn't too difficult to coordinate the logistics. The KT team was helping us from their end to make sure the reporters would confirm their attendance. We had a military media attaché working at the Governor's Palace – his name was Philip. I couldn't pull it off without Philip's assistance. Philip was instrumental to the success of media outreach day by assisting us with communication with the reporters. My job was to mentor DG Karimi with his speech and how he was going to break down the list of projects that had been implemented in Maiwand. The Maiwand Director of Education was involved in the media event because through our CA team we were going to donate 250 school bags to the children. On top of the school bags, the CA team built a school library and the library was going to be inaugurated. Our military counterparts built a soccer field. The soccer field was completed in time for the media day outreach. DG Karimi wanted to also show to the reporters the progress we had made with the VTC masonry and tailoring classes, the Model Farm at the Agriculture Center, and the upcoming government housing site for the Tashkiel workers. It was important for our BSO and DG Karimi to coordinate the security if we were going to walk around the Hutal area. The BSO, DG Karimi, and DST got together to discuss how we were going to do it and which sites we would visit first. Below is the agenda for the media that we prepared:

- DG Karimi holds his press conference in the DG's building.
- DG Karimi takes the press throughout the District Center.

- DG Karimi demonstrates the progress made at the Model Farm.
- DG Karimi demonstrates the progress made at the VTC (Masonry and Tailoring classes). The Masonry included the expansion of the DG's building entrance, noise generator wall, and model farm composting pit wall. The Tailoring classes included a demonstration of the Afghan flag the trainees have made for the Afghan ANP checkpoints.
- Walk through the Old British Fort.
- DG Karimi demonstrates the potential government housing.
- DG Karimi takes the press to the Hutal School to distribute the school bags and opens the library.
- DG Karimi takes the press to the new soccer field.
- After the walk around and demonstration of projects, DG Karimi invites the press back to his building for more questions and chai (tea).

Five days before the media day we reviewed the tentative agenda with DG Karimi. We ran into a problem with the invitees because the Director for Media in Kandahar City called off his participation. Apparently, the PG wanted him and the reporters to be somewhere else. I was extremely worried about this cancellation because we put in so much effort to coordinate the logistics and preparations for each site that the press was going to visit. For instance, we decorated the VTC with Afghan flags and the Model Farm was decorated with agricultural products. We were planning to have the agriculture trainers do a demonstration to the press. The Maiwand Director of Education was planning to have a small ceremony for the press. At this ceremony, DG Karimi would give a speech to the children to open the school year and distribute the school bags. We had the military flight arranged and everything look good from that end. The military air flight operations team knew the importance of media day and we were just happy that they would support us with the air movement. I already explained before how difficult it could be to get a military flight arranged for one day pick up and drop off. I called the Director for Media in

Kandahar City to discuss how we could make this work and get the reporters to Maiwand. He told me that he couldn't come, and hung up the phone. He was a bit rude. I told the news to DG Karimi and he came to my COP to call the Director for Media. When DG Karimi called the Director for Media, he was treated the same way I was. I knew that if we didn't make this happen, I wasn't sure when we would have another opportunity. One of my colleagues from Area A found out about the possible cancellation of the event. My colleague knew the PG and personally sent an email asking him if he would allow the press to come to Maiwand. The PG didn't think twice and ordered the media to be present at the event. Not only was the PG allowing the press to go to Maiwand, he also gave permission to his Deputy Provincial Governor to come to Maiwand and represent him. I was so happy to hear the news and from there nothing would stop us!

The day before media day we ran a rehearsal with DG Karimi and we walked around the sites where we would take the media. All school bags were in place and ready for distribution. Each school bag had pens and a notebook. The soccer field was cleaned. The VTC trainees were going to be present to do a demonstration for the press and Deputy Provincial Governor. I was very tired from doing the coordination but I knew I would be satisfied after the event. This event was important for the district strategically because Maiwand had such a bad image among Kandaharis as an insecure district that demonstrating to the media that the community is coming together to work on development was a sign of prosperity. It was a sign that things were changing in Maiwand for the better.

On media day, as we had done before, my military counterparts and I greeted the press when they landed in our COP Helicopter Landing Zone. Afterwards, we walked to the District Center in order for the press and Deputy Provincial Governor to meet DG Karimi. DG Karimi went ahead with his press conference in the conference room. At the press conference, DG

Karimi highlighted the 2011 development projects with a joint cooperation with the Afghan government, military counterparts, and DST. I was so proud of our DG and was impressed with his leadership to lead the press conference. When he was giving his speech, I thought about on the days when I first came to Maiwand and everyone was talking about his removal. And after eight months, he had changed so much, mostly because of our mentorship. We never stopped with the mentorship and continued to hammer away every day and night to make sure DG Karimi continued to improve in his role. After the press conference, DG Karimi went ahead with the agenda and took the press and Deputy Provincial Governor to the sites outlined under the agenda. When we stopped by the VTC, the program manager presented an Afghan flag, made by our trainees, to the Deputy Provincial Governor, DG Karimi, and other visitors from our chain of command. The Deputy Provincial Governor congratulated DG Karimi for his outstanding presentation at the press conference and for his ongoing effort to support technical training, which could generate future employment. The farmers at the Model Farm participated in a small demonstration. When we reached the school, I was blown away to see so many children waiting in line to greet DG Karimi, Deputy Provincial Governor, and the press. The Deputy Provincial Governor spoke to the children and teachers and told them how important it was to go to school. Illiteracy in Maiwand was high and it was important for the children to attend school. DG Karimi told the children the importance of school because they were the future of Maiwand. After the speeches, one student performed an Afghan recital to commemorate the special and symbolic day. Following the recital, the school principal took the invitees to the brand new school library. After the visit, DG Karimi took questions from the local reporters and the New York Times. DG Karimi answered all the questions asked and the reporters were pleased by how active DG Karimi was in Maiwand. The media day event lasted for an entire day, from 9:00 am to 3:00 pm. On this day, Maiwand was the spotlight for the media. On this day, Maiwand demonstrated to the Afghan government that development is taking place and that it is safe to visit. On this day, DG Karimi demonstrated that he could lead the district. On this day, the DST demonstrated that it could mentor DG Karimi and that, with perseverance and dedication, governance and development could work in Maiwand. On this day, we concluded our one-year strategy to bring the Line Ministry Directors to discuss development, then bring the rule of law officials, and then the media. All three events served the purpose to build the governance development efforts in Maiwand. Now it was time for the next phase, which would be the toughest one: Following up on the promises made by the Afghan officials. As I already mentioned once before, it is easy to make promises, but it is important to make sure that the promises are kept. Media day was held in the third week of September. Many of us would run out of time to continue with the follow-ups and I knew that the next step would be for my replacement to follow up, along with the DG.

Following the media day, the DST and Samsung distributed comic books to the students at the Hutal school. We wanted to build on the momentum of the media day. The comic books encouraged the women to take disputes to the Jirgas and sent the message that women have legal rights under the Afghan Constitution. A Jirga is similar to a formal town meeting. We also distributed booklets with pictures of rural Afghanistan and various U.S. Embassy educational posters. The posters included a world almanac, scientific and astronomical charts, and poetry. All the posters were written in Dari, Pashto, and English. The Hutal School Principal and teachers welcomed this effort and thanked the DST and Samsung for engaging with the students.

The media day week was full of happy surprises. That same week, the U.S. Embassy notified me that the grant proposal that we submitted to start up a carpentry course was approved. I was so happy that another NGO would do the project and that we were going to expand the VTC. This was a positive sign because it demonstrated that gradually we were making ground on the development effort. As I mentioned before, I wanted to start the project small and see how it would work. Gradual progress is more important than trying to do too much and making it too big. If you remember, at the beginning of 2011, no NGO wanted to come to Maiwand. Now after seeing the success at the VTC, more NGOs showed signs of interest of working in Maiwand. I asked the NGO to send the program manager to discuss the carpentry course. When the program manager came to the COP to discuss the logistics of the project, he was high on drugs. You can tell when someone was high on drugs. He was acting very mellow, his eyes were red, and his mouth was dried. Because drug use is common in Afghanistan, I was never surprised if someone was on drugs. As soon as the NGO representative left the COP I knew I wasn't going to use them as an implementing partner. I would not put taxpayers' money at risk on people that didn't take their work seriously. It was sad because we put so much effort into the preparation of the proposal and at the end we had to cancel the project. There was no fallout from dropping this NGO since we didn't promise anything to the NGO or the community yet. One thing that I knew is that now we had more leverage and interest by NGOs to do work in Maiwand. Now it was a matter of waiting until the next fiscal year started to work with another NGO to do the carpentry course.

We continued to move forward with small successes. The first week of October we graduated the first masonry class. It was symbolic because the graduation demonstrated a long year's work to complete the first development small grant project organized and led by Afghans. DG Karimi was pleased to see the completion of the DST Maiwand VTC Masonry course. DG Karimi requested the elders and local businesses to hire the masons for potential projects. DG Karimi distributed "Certificates of Completion" to 15 Masonry Graduates at a symbolic ceremony before the Tribal Elders. DG Karimi spoke on the importance of technical training in reducing the unemployment and poverty rates and the need for commitment to hire these graduates. His comments were in line with the Labor Ministry's statement that 85% of the people who receive technical and professional training go on to find jobs. Following the ceremony, the DST and BSO issued CERP microgrants of $500 to each graduate for their business start-up outlays. The DST and DG Karimi thanked WP for believing in Maiwand as this was the first NGO to complete a project in there. Through its implementing partner, WP, the DST donated flower vases to decorate the completed entranceway of the District Center, and DG Karimi thanked the DST and WP for beautifying it. In addition to learning basic skills, these graduates had multiple "on-the-job" training projects, which included construction of a noise barrier, refurbishment of the entrance way at the District Center, building a generator foundation, fixing the District Governor's security building bathroom, and building a composting pit wall at the Model Farm. Leveraging on the impact of this training, our masons' linkage to these construction projects provided them with a livelihood, and demonstrated our collective commitment to the community.

Following the ceremony to recognize our masons, internally we wanted to recognize our military counterparts that have helped us so much with the DST governance and development efforts. I thought it was important to show appreciation to those that have helped us so much throughout the year. We couldn't have done it without them. Our work in Maiwand was done as a team and it wasn't individualistic. Working as a team was an important aspect of my work there and this was my first priority when I arrived. Before, there was no team spirit, which stalled the district in 2010 with regard to governance and development. Our military counterparts worked tirelessly to improve the lives of Maiwands. Their dedication, professionalism, and clear understanding of development will be felt for years to come. The DST told our military counterparts that they should all feel proud of the work that we had done in Maiwand. We built the governance and development foundation for our successors to follow. To my military counterparts, thank you for believing in Maiwand. It was also a sad moment for me personally because I felt my work was coming to an end. My military counterparts had two more months of work and I had three more months.

By early October, I had to make my decision if I wanted to extend for another year's tour in Afghanistan. The people in Area A were pleased with the work I did in Maiwand and how I turned around the district. Now it was time for me to move on or continue to work in Afghanistan. I began to think about it beginning in summer 2011. I'd been doing this type of work since 2008, first in Iraq and then Afghanistan. I knew that I had to take care of my personal life. I knew that there was something that I was missing. I didn't want to spend the rest of my thirties in a war zone and I knew that I wanted to do something different and be somewhere where I could continue to grow professionally. I didn't have enough words to say thank you to the opportunity the State Department provided me to work in Iraq and Afghanistan. I proudly served America to change people's lives in conflict nations. I served at the other "front" of the war, which was to bring good governance and development. Developing local policy on the front lines was an enriching experience, but I knew that it was time to come home and do something different. I knew that it was time to serve at the other front, which is in America. I was getting burned out and very tired. I knew that I needed a break and I felt my brain was asking for this break. I told my colleagues at Area A that I wasn't going to extend. My colleagues at Area A respected my decision and thanked me for my service. They knew how much effort and dedication I put into my work. I demonstrated discipline and I always stayed positive, even in dark times. I think this is one of the things that set me apart. I always tried to send encouragement, which allowed me to see the light at the end of the tunnel. By mid-October, I was seeing many lights in Maiwand after a long year of work. When I first came to Maiwand there was no light at the end of the tunnel. Through my perseverance I began to discover the light in Maiwand. In this environment you could stay negative; that is easy because the environment could feed discouragement. Afghanistan is not an easy place in which to work. The country functions very slow and things didn't happen that quickly. When you come to Afghanistan you have to have a different approach. I lowered my expectations and was very cautious on how I approached and moved forward in the district. In the end, I had no regrets about the work that I'd done in Maiwand. I knew that October was probably going to be the last month to do something in Maiwand. Very soon I would leave for my last R&R and then come back in mid-November. I knew when I came back in November I would only have two months left to work in Maiwand. I knew that when I came back my role would be more as a mentor to the new folks at the DST and it would be up to the new DST members to continue with our success.

Continuing with our long year strategy, it was time now to do the follow-ups. After all the visits by the provincial authorities that we brought to Maiwand, it was time to see if they were going to deliver to the district. I knew this was going to be a big test for all of us. It was time to see what the Afghan government officials could do for Maiwand. The Afghan Chief Judge promised Maiwand that they would support it with a judicial center, judge and attorney general. Maiwand had a judge but he sat in Kandahar City and never came to Maiwand. Maiwand didn't have an attorney general. We brought back the Afghan Judicial Officials to speak with DG Karimi and DCOP to discuss a way forward with rule of law. This time the logistics were taken care of by the KT rule of law team, which was a big relief for me because it takes so much time to do the coordination. Now, it was only a matter of waiting for the Afghan Judicial Officials to come to Maiwand. Similar to other VIP visits, in the days before the meeting I would meet with DG Karimi to discuss the agenda and talking points. DG Karimi knew that this meeting was more of a follow up and it was important to pressure the Afghan Judicial Officials to provide Maiwand with a judicial center, judge, and attorney general. Mentorship and preparation was an important part of my job and I built a good relationship with DG Karimi. When the visitors came to Maiwand, we took the Chief Judge to the District Center to meet with DG Karimi and DCOP. At the District Center, the Chief Judge discussed the possible site for the judicial center. DG Karimi proposed to use of one of the empty buildings at the Agriculture Center, which could serve as the judicial center. The only logistical work that needed to be done was the transfer of the land where the building sat from the Ministry of Agriculture to the Ministry of Justice. The Chief Judge visited the building at the Agriculture Center and he was very impressed with it. The Chief Judge promised to send a land recorder from the Ministry of Justice to record the land. The Chief Judge informed DG Karimi that he hoped to provide a judge sometime by late December. The judge that was assigned for Maiwand was dismissed because of his lack of effort in coming to Maiwand. There was a shortage of judges in Afghanistan and we all knew that when new judges come to a province, they would usually go to the large districts and Maiwand wasn't a large district. Or the judges just didn't want to travel to the district because of the security. DG Karimi told the Chief Judge that the judge should feel secure coming to Maiwand and that strong security would be provided. The Chief Judge agreed that the Hutal area where the District Center and potential judicial center were located was secure. Another matter that was discussed was the appointment of an attorney general for Maiwand to prosecute political cases related to criminal acts. With no judge and attorney general it put the district in an awkward situation because people that got arrested for drugs could probably get released in a few days or be transferred to Kandahar City. Eventually they would get released because of lack of paper work to prosecute the criminal. Therefore, it was important that we assigned, at least on a part-time basis, an attorney general. The

Chief Judge promised DG Karimi that he would work with the Provincial Attorney General to assign the Zharay District Attorney General to Maiwand. The Zharay Attorney General would visit Maiwand for two days each week and would be present during the arrests. Additionally, he would push for the proper paperwork to be done in order to prosecute criminals. Zharay is a district located next to Maiwand. The Arghandab Attorney General never showed an interest in coming to Maiwand. The visitors left in good spirits and DG Karimi was still skeptical about the promises by the Chief Judge. A week later, the Ministry of Justice land recorder came to Maiwand to record the land of the potential judicial center and the Zharay attorney general came to Maiwand and expressed his support to assist with the prosecution of cases. I was very pleased these things happened and the Chief Judge was able to deliver on his promises. It was symbolic. I began to see more lights at the end of the tunnel. With perseverance we continued to see more success.

By the end of the first week of October, I inspected the completion of the Chelgazi hand water well pumps. We promised DG Karimi that after the GIRoA Outreach Shura, we would do a small project in Chelgazi. (I mentioned this GIRoA Outreach Shura before under the May section.) It took a while to complete the project because the contractor couldn't finish the project on time. We funded two hand water well pumps. My military counterparts and I walked to Chelgazi to inspect them. Before we made a payment, we wanted to double check and see that they existed and were functional. The wells would impact more than 45 families in the Chelgazi village. DG Karimi was pleased with the completion of the project and the villagers welcomed the assistance to Chelgazi. Afghans complained a lot about the lack of water and we hoped that providing the two wells could help mediate the problem for the Chelgazi village. We hoped that the project would begin to change the perception among the local population of DG Karimi and they would see him as someone who was trying to help with their needs.

I mentioned that our VTC tailoring trainees were making Afghan flags for the Afghan ANP checkpoints. We had a small request by our BSO to make a large Afghan flag for the Flying J. The Flying J was a truck stop built on highway 1. It had a large Afghan flagpole. The VTC trainees made the large Afghan flag and presented the flag to DG Karimi. After the Wednesday People's Shura, DG Karimi, DST, and our BSO drove to the Flying J and we all helped DG Karimi raise the Afghan Flag. DG Karimi saluted the Afghan flag. I was so happy to see that the DST was contributing to projects and we were supporting DG Karimi and the military.

One of the big problems was that we lacked a functional Tashkiel. The Tashkiel were the Afghan government civil servants. Maiwand only had Tashkiel workers under the health, agriculture, civil registry, telecommunication, education, and energy. Only the health, education, and civil registry workers were busy working in the district. The other workers didn't do much work. The Tashkiel workers didn't work because they were not being challenged by their respective ministries. If the ministry didn't task or resource the Tashkiel worker, then the Tashkiel worker would not know what to do. And this is what happened in Maiwand. For instance, I spoke with the telecommunications worker and he told me that he didn't come to work because he didn't know what to do. The Provincial Director of Telecommunication sits in the Kandahar City. He never came to Maiwand and would not instruct their reps in the district about their duties. A similar thing happened to the agriculture officer. We had two agriculture officers but only one came every now and then to the Agriculture Center. The other agriculture officer disappeared and nobody knew his whereabouts. When the Canadians donated the Agriculture Center to the Maiwand, the Provincial Director of Agriculture for Kandahar Province promised them that they would provide all the necessary resources to have a functional Agriculture Center and the agriculture Tashkiel would be filled. Unfortunately, these promises never happened. To provide a short remedy to this problem, USAID had the District Delivery Program (DDP), which would assist to fill the Tashkiel, and workers would receive danger pay on their salaries. The DDP plan had been working in other districts. It was run by the Independent Directorate of Local Governance (IDLG) and the IDLG plays an instrumental part in the hiring process of the Afghan civil servants. The IDLG would visit a district, make an assessment, and then determine the feasibility to have a DDP program in the district. The second week of October the IDLG came to Maiwand to spend two days in the district and make sure the people's problems were in line with what DG Karimi was reporting.

It was time for Maiwand to have an IDLG assessment visit. We had been waiting for this visit since March 2011. I didn't know why it took so long for the assessment team to come to Maiwand but I knew I would not see this program running, because by the time the IDLG hired Tashkiel workers, I would be in the states for good. Just like the other VIP visits that we had, we had to prepare DG Karimi on the upcoming IDLG visit. DG Karimi had to make a presentation on the governance and development strategy for Maiwand and its critical needs. As you could tell, mentorship was a strong component of my job as the lead governance advisor. I had to brief DG Karimi on his main priorities for the district and how he wanted the key Line Ministries to assist Maiwand. DG Karimi and I knew that just filling a Tashkiel was not appropriate if the Tashkiel workers were not tasked and resourced. Otherwise, the new Tashkiel workers would just sit in an empty office doing nothing. I didn't have to organize the logistics for this trip. All the logistics were organized by the Regional Command South. Our role was to support the IDLG team by providing them with security, taking them to the District Center, and assisting DG Karimi on organizing a two-day workshop with the Maiwand Tashkiel workers and key tribal leaders. On the day of the visit, we took the

IDLG team to the District Center and the team met with DG Karimi. DG Karimi and the IDLG had a long discussion on what the IDLG could do for Maiwand through the DDP program. I was present at the meeting and DG Karimi told the IDLG team that it was important that the ministry resource and task their respective workers; otherwise, he didn't really see the impact. The IDLG understood where DG Karimi was coming from and welcomed his comment as valuable. After the long meeting, the IDLG team met with the Maiwand's Tashkiel workers. The IDLG went forward with the two-day workshop. The IDLG did a good job engaging with the key leaders and Maiwand Tashkiel workers. They broke into groups to discuss the different sectors such as education, agriculture, political moderation and stable governance, safe and secure environment, rule of law, sustainable economy, and service delivery. In each group, members spoke about the problem and how they could work together to address the needs. On the second day, all the groups got together and discussed openly how the IDLG could help address the people's needs and what positions were the priority to fill.

Some of the key needs expressed by sector areas were as follows:

a. Education – Build more schools as long as security could be provided.
b. Agriculture – Greenhouse construction, saffron production, and livestock.
c. Public Health – Clinic expansion, better medications, and treatment of drug abusers.
d. MRRD – Water, sanitation, and road construction.

The breakout group exercise demonstrated the elders' enthusiasm and sense of ownership about their community's problems. As we moved towards transition, strengthening the linkages between community stakeholders and line ministries would become more critical to aligning resources and to channel Afghan funding to projects. I was pleased with the two-day workshop because I never saw my Afghan counterparts so involved and eager to work on the problem in an open manner.

Throughout the year we continued with the radio program *Local Democracy Voices*. As you may know, *Local Democracy Voices* was the first project we did. The radio program was one of a kind in Maiwand because it focused on educating the people on governance and development issues. We added more content to the radio station. We began to send rule of law and public health messages. The rule of law messages fell under the rule of law stabilization effort and the component was informal. For instance, in one week the rule of law stabilization informal topic was "Dispute between kids and parents on forced marriage." The program addressed the fathers of Amena and Jamshaid who were brothers and had engaged their kids when they were babies. Now these two kids are 14 and 15 years old. They strongly disagree with their engagement but their parents were trying to force them to marry. Amena is very sad and reluctant to marry. Both families resolved their dispute between the kids and parents through a Jirga. On public health, we sent messages on polio, diarrhea, and tuberculosis. The Afghan Ministry of Public Health approved all public health messages. I was very pleased with the radio message effort because it added to the good work that we were doing in Maiwand. Our PSYOPS team continued to provide radios to the local population so they could tune in.

The week before I left on R&R, I was eating lunch by the Gazebo and, as I finished my food, I could see the DCOP walking alone. I asked myself why he would be walking on his own with no escort? I was eating lunch with Scramble. I told him that we must find out what is going on. As I was getting closer to the DCOP, I noticed something on his face. I couldn't see well and when he got closer, half of his face was bleeding. I asked him what went wrong and he told me he was in a shootout with some insurgents. Some of his cops got hurt and he brought them inside the COP so we could take a look at them. The DCOP looked very bad and just seeing him bleed was another reminder that I was in war zone. It was very common to hear the medical helicopter landing on our COP to pick up an Afghan who either was badly injured or dead. I saw many body bags going inside the medial helicopter throughout my tour. But you just get used to that; it becomes normal and it just is what it is. You remember that you are in a war zone and that you need to take care of yourself.

By the third week of October I was ready to take my last R&R. This time I had no real drama leaving the COP. The U.S. Embassy Air helicopter came to pick me up and took me to KAF, where I waited a couple of days before I left for America. The next time, I would be leaving Afghanistan for good. I left Maiwand a little sad and although I knew the past three months were difficult, and we experienced a lot of challenges, deep inside I knew that it was probably the last time I would have this level of experience. I knew when I came back things would be a bit different. My military colleagues that I'd worked with the entire year would be getting ready to leave to come home and I knew I would be following right after. For some reason, every time I left for America something bad happened in Maiwand and my military counterparts always joke with me on this. Before I left on my last R&R the Sergeant Major for the Battalion told me that he hoped things would remain calm during my absence. Well, guess what, the curse would continue because there was a big change in my district that impacted my work. I will elaborate on this change later. I wanted to use my last break to reflect on the work that we did over the year because I knew things would change soon. I say change because I knew when I came back I would be thinking coming home, on my way out of Maiwand. I would spend my last holidays away from home. I also wanted to take the opportunity to think about whether or not I made the right decision on not extending. However, deep inside, I knew it was time for me to go and close this chapter of my life. If the Embassy had to tell me that I would not come back to Maiwand anymore then I would leave Maiwand with no regrets. We turned around a district. We put Maiwand in the spotlight among Afghan and American policymakers. We made people believe again in Maiwand. We made Maiwand a strong district. We won the hearts and minds and trust from my Afghan counterparts. Building trust was part of the success of my work. The fact that we didn't have many resources available pushed us to do a lot of critical thinking to figure out a way to help our Afghan counterparts. We did it and now it was time for our successors to continue with what we built. And so I left Afghanistan on a long flight from Kandahar to Dubai to America.

Talking to the masonry trainees on the importance of the training.

Monitoring the work of the masons at the Police Center. Building a noise generator wall.

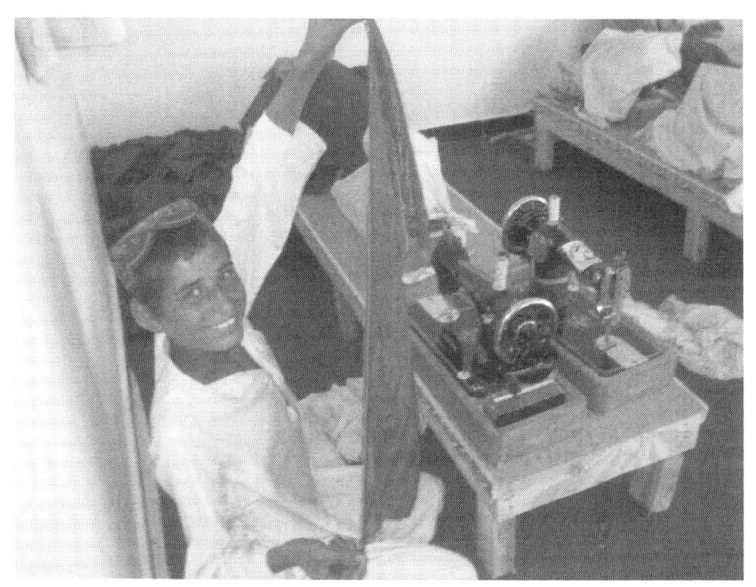

Our proud tailor demonstrates his Afghan flag.

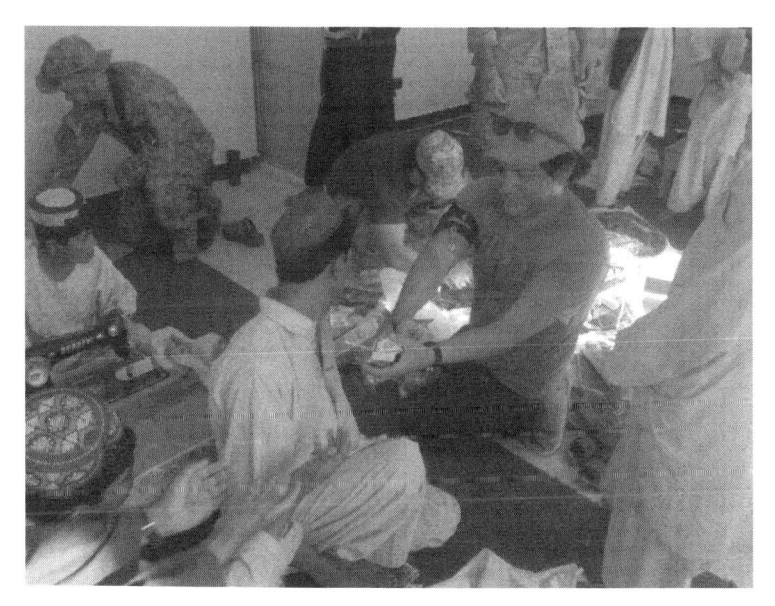

Providing humanitarian assistance to the tailoring trainees. Thanks to our military counterparts for providing us with the supplies.

The masons building the DG's building entrance.

First symbolic graduation for masons in Maiwand. DG Karimi giving out the certificates.

Afghan officials visit the VTC tailoring class.

Our mason graduate receives a CERP micro-grant to open his business.

With the students from the Hutal School.

Distributing education rule of law comic books to the students at the Hutal School.

Completion of Chelgazi hand water well pump.

Symbolic media day in Maiwand and at the Hutal School.

Donating education posters to the Hutal School.

At media day, the Provincial Deputy Governor and DG distributing school bags to the student.

DG Karimi working with the Afghan IDLG central government representatives on the priorities for Maiwand to fill his Tashkiel.

Maiwand's Director of Education explaining to the IDLG the educational needs for the schools.

Scouting for insurgent threat.

With my team walking in rural Hutal.

VI

TRANSITION

I came back to Afghanistan in the middle of November. I booked a helicopter flight the day after I landed in KAF because I wanted to come back right away to Maiwand. I knew I didn't have that much time left. Scramble was in Area A for a training and I asked him if something tragic happened during my absence. He told me that nothing bad happened. Before I left, Scramble took the lead to graduate the tailors from the VTC. He briefed me on the preparation for the ceremony. Scramble and my military counterparts worked on the small business micro-grant applications, which we promised we would provide to the trainees after they graduated. With the micro-grant money the tailor graduates would be able to buy more sewing machines and open their own businesses. For those opting to defer their business start-up plans, the best efforts were made to find suitable apprenticeships. This allowed our graduates to strengthen their skills, provide them a livelihood, and demonstrate our ongoing collective commitment to the community. On the day of the ceremony, DG Karimi distributed "Certificates of Completion" to 25 tailoring graduates. DG Karimi congratulated the students and asked them about what they learned and if they promised to go to work. He told them that he didn't want to see them wandering around the bazaar. DG Karimi spoke of the importance of technical training in reducing the unemployment and poverty rates and the need for more vocational training courses to be offered. His comments were in accord with the recent IDLG Assessment Team visitors who welcomed the DST Vocational Training

Initiative as it supported Maiwand's Five Year District Development Plan and had been vetted by the community. In addition to receiving a Certificate of Completion, each graduate received a sewing machine. I was so pleased to hear that everything went well. Scramble and I put a lot of effort on this project and I was sad also to see that it was the last project on which Scramble and I would work together. Scramble completed his tour in Maiwand and would not be back to Maiwand. I didn't have his replacement yet so I would be alone running the DST for a bit. But it wasn't a big deal as I'd done it before. As a leader, I expressed gratitude and satisfaction with all the work Scramble had provided over a year in Maiwand. Scramble and I had our differences but we worked it out and we had a good strong team. We mentored each other and we both cared for our assignment and were serious about turning around the district. We knew we were going to have challenges and we supported each other as much as we could. We were the only civilian experts in our COP and we always tried to make sure we had good communication and coordination to lead the DST to success. We *did* lead the DST to success. I was happy that I didn't have any bad news so far. That was great. But not so fast!!

I left to Maiwand on a Tuesday. Scramble came to the flight line to say goodbye. I landed on my COP around 10:00 am in the morning. Things remained calm and I went to my trailer and started to unpack. I was jetlagged and wanted to take a rest. But before that, I wanted to say hello to my military counterparts. I went to the governance operations room to say hello. People were all smiles and suddenly an email came through just as I was entering the room. DG Karimi was going to be replaced by a new DG (I would call the new District Governor – DG Salim). We all knew DG Karimi was going to be removed. That wasn't a surprise. I heard the rumor that DG Karimi was going to be removed since the first day I got to Maiwand. The rumor died as DG Karimi continued to show progress. DG Karimi had been in Maiwand serving as the District Governor since 2009, which is a long time in Afghan terms. The DG's are appointed and these are no-limit terms. Deep inside I knew DG Karimi was burned out and wanted to move on and be with his family. I think we did a good job mentoring him and that he would be wiser and would have more tools to make his job easier in the next phase of his career. DG Karimi and I were very close and we developed a good working relationship. We respected each other. I was very angry about how the PG removed DG Karimi. The PG had the right to decide when the DG could be removed and how he would be removed. DG Karimi was told to leave Maiwand the next day, Wednesday. Yes, leaving the next day, which didn't leave time for a turnover from one DG to another DG. I thought it was important for DG Salim to learn from DG Karimi on how to interact with the key powerbrokers, elders, military, community, and DST. If you allowed DG Karimi to leave the next day, DG Karimi would take all the knowledge with him. It was a big setback for the district. I am very critical of the PG because I think he made a horrible decision regarding how to remove DG Karimi. We all knew that DG Karimi was going to be removed but I was more upset with the procedure than the action. DG Salim came to Maiwand Tuesday night, the same Tuesday that I arrived in Maiwand. The next day at a People's Shura DG Karimi was going to introduce DG Salim to the people, military, and the DST. I went to the District Center early Wednesday morning to say hello to DG Karimi and he gave me a big hug when he saw me. DG Karimi looked sad and a bit confused because his replacement came too soon with no real turn over time. Well in politics you didn't have a real turn over. In a normal government administration you have staff to support you and close advisors. In rural Afghanistan, the District Governor doesn't really have a stable government administration and close technical advisors. There wasn't much we could do and I thanked DG Karimi for the excellent work he did as DG in Maiwand and wished him all the best. DG Karimi introduced DG Salim to everyone. I welcomed DG Salim to

Maiwand and offered our friendship and collaboration. I knew I would not have enough time to work with DG Salim because in 7 weeks I would be on my way out. DG Salim came to Maiwand when almost all key players from the military and the DST were about to leave, which meant that projects would come to an end and we would all be getting ready to welcome our replacements. DG Salim didn't know what was coming soon but no matter what; I knew I would do my best to make his job easier. But it would also be difficult because in this environment you have to get to know the person informally and formally. It took me a couple of months before DG Karimi, the military, and the DST developed a good working relationship. I knew with DG Salim it would take some time before we had something on the ground to develop.

Nobody knew much about DG Salim's personality and his plans for Maiwand. Now, it was time to begin to work with the mentorship and make sure that Maiwand continued with the governance and development efforts. DG Karimi left Maiwand on a Wednesday and I was looking forward to getting to know the new DG. When DG Karimi introduced me to DG Salim I didn't get a good vibe from DG Salim. DG Salim was very cold and looked angry. He wasn't from Maiwand and he would have big shoes to fill because he had to build a strong relationship with the Maiwand tribal elders and powerbrokers. Change is always good and I welcomed change. When there is change you have new ideas, new strategies, you test what worked before or what didn't, you do lessons learned, and you can reinvent yourself. I took the positive side on having a new DG. But I knew that having DG Salim in place would slow our efforts a little bit because he would need time to get adjusted with the district. As his governance advisor, I advised him to take things slowly and take his time to get to know how the system works and what has been done before. It was important for him to know what had been done before so he didn't reinvent the wheel. I told him that good time management would make the most use of the resources that he would have. I wanted to know what his intentions were for the district and how he wanted to move forward. It was also important to see what kind of a relationship he was going to have with the local population and with us. I was a bit worried about the district because I wasn't sure what direction it would take now that we had DG Salim, especially now that more changes were coming to the district.

When I came back to the COP on Wednesday after meeting DG Salim, I sat alone on my chair and began to think about how I was going to approach the new change. I wasn't prepared for the new changes; nobody was. Nobody was given the time to prepare for DG Salim. It was important to continue with mentorship of DG Salim on how to make local policy across the spectrum of economic, administrative, and social areas. The intent was to continue to improve governance performance and development, and increase public sector effectiveness. Good governance in Maiwand meant a competent management of the district's resources and affairs in a manner that was open, transparent, accountable, and responsive to the people's needs. But I knew that it would be a matter of time for DG Salim to get adjusted and, by the time this happened, I would not be in Maiwand. This was going to be the task for my replacement.

The following days were a bit slow. We just concluded the VTC and with DG Salim new in his office, we didn't want to start a new project that quick. As the days passed, my time in Maiwand was getting shorter. Soon, it was Thanksgiving in Maiwand. This was going to be my last Thanksgiving overseas. We had a great Thanksgiving and I ate Thanksgiving dinner with my military counterparts. We were like a family. Our families, friends, and loved ones were back home in the States while we were in Afghanistan in the middle of nowhere. We had turkey, mashed potatoes, pumpkin pie, and ice cream. I always looked forward to a good dinner because they didn't come to the COP very often. Not that the food was horrible all the time. I got used to the food that we ate but a nice dinner was always welcome. When I came back to my trailer I did some reflection and thanked God for giving me good health while in Afghanistan. I was a bit sad that I wasn't with my family. I didn't celebrate Christmas but I took Thanksgiving seriously. I wanted to watch the Thanksgiving Parade over the Internet but couldn't. I watched a Christmas movie and went to bed. The next day it was just another day in Maiwand.

I met with my military counterparts to discuss how we would mentor DG Salim. Since DG Karimi left with all the knowledge, it was our role to provide DG Salim with the proper knowledge and put him up to speed. Our team informed DG Salim on the governance and development progress that had been made over the year with the military, USAID, U.S. Embassy Funds, and Afghan government. DG Salim welcomed the mentorship. I advised DG Salim on the importance of engaging with the key Line Ministry Directors and the need for follow-ups. This was the first time DG Salim was a District Governor and I wanted him to be well aware of how we worked with the Kandahar Provincial Authorities. DG Salim told me that he would engage with the key Afghan ministries such as MRRD, Agriculture, and Education. I advised DG Salim on the upcoming 1391 budget approval and that it would be important for him to engage with the Provincial Director of Economy who also chairs the Provincial Development Council to discuss possible ways for Maiwand to get development assistance. DG Salim agreed with the DST that it was important for the Afghan government to provide development funding. It was important for the DST to guide DG Salim in developing the skills to lead the District. So, for the next few weeks, the DST continued to mentor DG Salim on how to:

- Enhance the district organization, technical, and management capacities for effective service delivery.
- Enhance financial management and district decentralization.
- Strengthen the planning and budgeting.
- Enhance community participation.

- Strengthen mechanisms for efficient coordination, monitoring, and evaluation.

Key areas of discussion for the next weeks were on:

- Filling the Tashkiel and USAID/DDP status.
- Updating on past and ongoing USAID projects.
- 1391 budget discussion with Director of Economy and Provincial Development Council Chairman.
- MRRD completion of 130 water wells.
- Re-establishing Community Development Councils.
- Follow-ups from the Governance and Rule of Law meetings organized this year. The DST informed DG Salim on the key Line Ministry Directors' visits such as Justice, MRRD, Economy, and Electricity.
- Preparation for Spring poppy eradication. Poppy harvest starts every Spring. Growing poppy is illegal in Afghanistan but the harvest is a multi-billion dollar trade. Some Taliban commanders deliberately delay the start of the Spring fighting so as to allow farmers a chance to complete the opium harvest.

The main objective for the DST was to continue to strengthen the district covered by adequate management resources (human, financial and material), aiming for efficient services delivery to citizens. I expected that it would take some time for DG Salim to be completely prepared for the administration of the district. DG Salim was aware of the arrest of the DDA Chairman and that, due to his arrest, the DDA had not been active since August. DG Salim was not pleased that the DDA was not active because he knew that the DDA Chairman played an important role in coordinating the development efforts. So his first priority was to re-elect a new DDA Chairman and Clerk. Two weeks later, DG Salim called for the re-election of the DDA Chairman and Clerk. I was pleased by this because it demonstrated his commitment to the development efforts. I mentioned to him the importance to have a DDA Chairman so we could move forward with development projects.

By December the elders were not talking so much about the DDA Chairman and Clerk who got arrested. With DG Salim the elders were upbeat and reignited the DDA.

By the middle of December, I realized I couldn't do much with DG Salim, DDA, and the other Afghan key partners. I realized that I was leaving soon and my role would fall on the mentorship side. The only thing that I could do with DG Salim was to prepare him as much as I could so he could have a smooth transition with the community in order for him to be an effective leader. Similar to what we did for media day, we took DG Salim around the projects that we had completed in Maiwand. DG Salim complained that nothing had been done in Maiwand and I told him that indeed many projects had been completed in Maiwand. This was a negative outcome from removing DG Karimi so quickly and not passing on the proper information to DG Salim. So now DG Salim had to learn everything from the ground and I didn't want him to reinvent the wheel. It was important for DG Salim not to think that nothing was done in Maiwand, because, in fact, many things were done with the community support. We took DG Salim to:

a. DST – VTC completed work (District Center entrance, repaired of bathrooms in front of DG's building, Police Center noise generator wall, and tailoring location).
b. Military reconstruction projects – Landscaping, government housing, soccer field, playground, Hutal school library, Afghan flag pole, and refurbishment of the District Police Center.
c. Hutal School – Completed work by the military and USAID. The DST informed DG Salim that the DST has assisted the Hutal school with school supplies that included informative scientific posters, rule of law comic books, and a fully-funded a literacy course.

DG Salim was pleased with the progress that had been made

in Maiwand, with a strong partnership between the community, Afghan government, the military, and the DST. The DST informed DG Salim about the upcoming plans to fill his Tashkiel and how the government housing units could provide strong incentive for Tashkiel workers to come and stay in Maiwand during the workweek. Over the course of the weeks, I'd gotten to know more and more about DG Salim. He seemed like he wanted to learn how to govern the district. I think I did my best in the very short time I was with him to provide him with all the necessary information for upcoming items that needed importance. But, to the contrary of my work with DG Karimi, I couldn't do much for DG Salim and I was on my way out of Afghanistan. By the middle of December, I began to reflect on all of my work in Afghanistan and I was getting sad because I felt I was closing a chapter in my life that had meant so much for my career. Working on international development in the field, with the conditions I had, was going to be unmatchable. But there wasn't much more I could do than just relax and let the transition move along. I only had three more weeks left in Afghanistan and Christmas was just around the corner.

 Christmas was over and I spent Christmas alone in my trailer, just like I did in Iraq. This Christmas wasn't that easy. Although I didn't believe much in Christmas, the feeling of the holidays was felt when I read the news online or watched the news and all they talked about was Christmas. As I was writing this, I was already counting the days until I could come back home. The Christmas dinner was not that great and nothing like the Thanksgiving dinner. We had a different military unit than the one that served us on Thanksgiving, so that meant new cookers. On the personal side, it is very difficult to deal with emotions when you are stuck in this bubble and know that you can't do much about it. My girlfriend broke up with me. You know a person that you love walked away and then you couldn't do much about it from this bubble where I was sitting. All I know is that the experience could make me stronger and wiser. I always tried to get something positive out of any experience. I had learned a lot, and learning how to be patient was an asset for my life in the coming months.

For a few days, I had been doing a lot of reflection and I couldn't deny that I am a little sad that I was leaving. Next, I would be in transit but that is pretty much logistical paperwork. From my end, my work had officially ended in Afghanistan. All the brainstorming, governance, and development efforts were completed. I was not happy about how I was leaving the district. I didn't see the district going back to what it was when I first got there, but I could see some potential setbacks. From my side, there was nothing I could do. I wanted to do more to help the Maiwand people. During my last Shura I said goodbye to everyone. I thought I was leaving with a well-earned respect among the Afghan elders. These were elders and not young kids, so for me it meant a lot. I thanked the elders and DG Salim for all of their support throughout my year in Maiwand. I got to know many of them and I heard many requests for water and electricity. I told them that I was taking with me, in my heart, all the good memories in Maiwand and that I would always treasure my experience with everyone. The elders were happy that I was leaving Maiwand because they knew I was going back home to see my family. Afghans really respect you if you respect the family. They understood that family was important. Some of my Afghan friends didn't know that I was leaving and wanted to give me souvenir gifts. I told them that it was fine. I already had enough souvenir gifts from an entire year working and living in Maiwand. But one Afghan friend, Mr. Mir Alam, told me that he would give me a nice Afghan flag to take to America. After the meeting, I stood outside the door and the elders continued to say goodbye. I took pictures with several of the elders. I really wanted to say goodbye to everyone because we had a large turnout of people that I knew. In the end, it was important for me to pay my respects to my Afghan friends and say the proper goodbye. Later in the afternoon, as I was entering my base and I saw Mr. Mir Alam waving at me. He presented me with a nice

Afghan flag. I thanked him for all of his efforts to continue to help the students. Mr. Mir Alam is the Deputy Director of Education.

It was January 12th, 2012, my last day in Maiwand. I woke up early, around 12:30 am, and couldn't go back to bed until 3:00 am. Then I woke up again at 5:30 am. Pending the weather, the Embassy flight would pick me up soon, in two and a half hours. For me, this was the end of my work in Afghanistan and it was time to continue to do something new. I put a lot effort into my work in Afghanistan. I took my work seriously and really wanted to help people. If I was here only for the money then I would've just sat and let the days go by without doing something productive. I came to Afghanistan because I was curious to know what the buzz was about the country. Why was Afghanistan not moving forward? Was it all Taliban? Were we to blame because we didn't do our lessons learned? Were we promoting good policy that was suitable to the culture? Was it really worth it?

As I began to reflect and decompress, I could tell you that Afghanistan is not moving forward because the Afghan government appears to be stuck and is too centralized. The President wants too much control and would not allow the provinces to make their own policy. Plus there is the corruption problem that I would not entrust millions of dollars into a ministry without having proper accountability controls. The Taliban is bad for the country and for security. Without strong security it would be difficult for development to take off. Because of the Taliban activities we weren't able to engage better in reconstruction projects. Education is important for the young generation but in rural areas where there is Taliban control, like around where I lived in Maiwand in the villages of Band I Timor, children were not allowed to go to school. This was a major setback for the young generation who would at some point lead the country. I guess the Taliban didn't acknowledge that. We needed to be a bit more flexible with the Afghan government in order for them to learn how to govern. Afghanistan remains an infant democracy and, just like infants, it can make mistakes. Our Afghan counterparts had to learn from their own mistakes and do their own lessons learned. But we were there to mentor them and guide them to success, so they could see lights at the end of the tunnel. If you ask me right now, if Afghanistan is really worth the fight, I would say yes but I would be cautious, because we need to be patient. We have done many things for the Afghan government but now it is up to the Afghan government to take the lead of the country. If you ask me the same question a couple of years from now, most likely I would still have the same opinion, but I could change, and that would depend on the Afghans. For now, the future for Afghanistan appears to look bleak. This is a decision based on what I've seen on the ground. I have observed the ineffectiveness from the top national level to the lowest district level. After ten years of war, we are still stuck in a small bubble in Maiwand. Even with all the promises that we were going to expand our secure bubble with a large force, we are still stuck. We are having difficulties holding operations so civilian experts like me could come in and do governance and development.

In the end, I wish all the best to the Maiwand people. To the Maiwand people:

- I hope your needs are heard by the Afghan President.
- Please don't let insurgents intimidate you.
- It is important that you support your children and they get educated.
- The Afghan youth will save the country from collapse.
- We couldn't do it all. Please understand that.

To the Afghan government:

- It is important that you create your own policies and have the willingness to listen to the people, because elders in places like Maiwand are looking for your leadership.

- If you take the initiative, people will begin to have faith in the system. Otherwise, districts like Maiwand will continue to feel isolated and they will take the other option: a shadow government run by the Taliban.
- Listen and observe, do good policy.
- The farmers need you, the people need you.
- And it is all on your hands…………..

With the Deputy Director of Education.

The last day of DG Karimi and with DG Salim.

With an ANA soldier.

An Afghan National Police truck.

My trailer in Maiwand where I lived during my Afghan tour.

The vest that protected my life during my tour in Afghanistan.

Saying goodbye to my Afghan counterparts.

VII

POST MAIWAND

Currently, I am in transit and have finally left Kandahar Province. I am at the Embassy doing out-processing. I will be in the Embassy for a couple of days before I finally depart to the United States next week. I have dropped off my protective gear. It was kind of strange giving away my bulletproof vest because it was such a part of my life for one year. I literally sweated in my bulletproof vest for a year and it protected my life. I have left Kandahar Province with my head held high. Before I left Kandahar Province, I did my out-processing with my boss. My boss was very happy and pleased with my performance. He knew that, with the minimal resources I had available, I was able to make the most in my district. In Kabul I didn't know anyone, so I could just relax and begin to reflect on my experience.

I am very calm when I look at my experience in Maiwand, and every hour and second that passes, Maiwand looks farther and farther away. As I already mentioned, I have no regrets when I look back at my experience. We won the hearts and minds in Maiwand. As a team we were able to turnaround a district on the brink of collapse. Nobody believed in Maiwand when I got there. My story is unique, if we take into consideration the place and the hard environment where we lived. But I still can't believe it is over and that it is time to move on. I am leaving concerned because I don't know what the future holds for Afghanistan. There are too many hurdles and I don't know if we have time to assist our Afghan counterparts. To change a system in Afghanistan will take a lot of years and maybe an entire generation. I don't know how much progress we can make by 2014. Post-2014, our presence in the districts might not be as large as it was before. I don't know how effective and how much of an impact we can make by 2014. But one thing that I know from my experience is to not lose hope, because as I saw light at the end of the tunnel for Maiwand, I can see lights at the end of the tunnel for Afghanistan. You need to have a good team of people to support you and your Afghan counterparts will collaborate. We still can do good work in Afghanistan. It is important that we stay positive and understand the system well, to make sure the impact is felt across all layers of the government system and the community. My experience has taught me that it is important to pay attention on the outputs and outcomes. The outcomes can be small. Small wins will probably have more impact in the long-term than large wins. I say this with strong confidence based on my experience in Iraq and Afghanistan. Let's not lose hope. We can still make it work with good policy and proper lessons learned. But we will see. It is up to the Afghan government to decide how the country will move forward.

I am leaving Afghanistan.

Thank you for reading my stories.

January 21st, 2012

Kabul, Afghanistan

ACRONYMS

ALP – Afghan Local Police
ANA – Afghan National Army
ANP – Afghan National Police
ANSF – Afghan National Security Forces
BSO – Battle Space Owner
CIDA – Canadian International Development Agency
CA – Civil Affairs
CERP – Commanders Emergency Response Program
CO – Commanding Officer
COP – Combat Operation Outpost
DCOP – District Chief of Police
DDA – District Development Assembly
DDP – District Delivery Program
DG – District Governor
DST – District Support Team
FOB – Forward Operating Base
GIRoA – Government of the Islamic Republic of Afghanistan
IDLG – Independent Directorate Local Governance
IED – Improvised Explosive Device
ISAF – International Security Assistance Force
KAF – Kandahar Air Field
KT – Kandahar Team
MRRD – Ministry Rural Rehabilitation and Development
NABDP – National Area Based Development Program
NDS – National Director of Security
NGO – Non-governmental Organization
PG – Provincial Governor
PRT – Provincial Reconstruction Team
PDC – Provincial Development Council
PSYOPS – Psychological Operations
R&R – Rest and Recuperation
USAID – U.S. Agency for International and Development
VTC – Vocational Training Center
WFP – World Food Program

ABOUT THE AUTHOR

Carlos Terrones is an international development practitioner who has worked in international development projects related to good governance and civil society in Eastern Europe, the Middle East, Asia, and Latin America. Carlos started his international development career as a U.S. Peace Corps volunteer. Most recently, he completed his U.S. Department of State tours successfully in Iraq and Afghanistan and was involved at the cutting edge of building their institutions. His education background has focused on how to run the public institutions effectively. Carlos has a Bachelors Degree from the George Washington University, a Masters Degree in Public Administration from Columbia University's School of International and Public Affairs (SIPA), and has also attended the Executive Education Program at Harvard University John F. Kennedy School of Government. This is his first book.

Made in the USA
San Bernardino, CA
17 January 2014